• *Pursuing Pastoral Excellence* •

PURSUING PASTORAL EXCELLENCE

Pathways to Fruitful Leadership

Paul E. Hopkins

 ALBAN

Herndon, Virginia
www.alban.org

The Alban Institute

2121 Cooperative Way, Suite 100

Herndon, VA 20171

Cover design by Signal Hill.

Library of Congress Cataloging-in-Publication Data

Hopkins, Paul E.
  Pursuing pastoral excellence : pathways to fruitful leadership / Paul Hopkins.
    p. cm.
  Includes bibliographical references and index.
  ISBN 978-1-56699-410-1 (alk. paper)
  1. Pastoral theology. 2. Excellence--Religious aspects--Christianity. I. Alban Institute. II. Title.
  BV4011.3.H665 2010
  253--dc22

                              2010049354

10   11   12   13   14   VG   5   4   3   2   1

• *Contents* •

• *Foreword* •

How do clergy find ways to sustain the passion and effectiveness of their call, season upon season, crisis upon crisis, pastoral call upon pastoral call, sermon upon sermon? More important, how do clergy "bear fruit that lasts"? How do those crisis responses, pastoral calls, sermons, and seasons of pastoring provide sustenance to congregations so that they will bear fruit well past the leader's tenure?

At the heart of his book is the gospel metaphor that weaves through the text: "You did not choose me but I chose you. And I appointed you to go and bear fruit, fruit that will last" (John 15:16). Paul Hopkins asks the question: How can a pastoral leader bear fruit that lasts? How can a ministry make a lasting difference?

In a time when pastoral burn-out and misconduct are too often front page news, Hopkins turns to seven pastors to teach us about enduring, faithful ministry. Through his careful listening—he is the kind of listener we all long for, and long to be—Hopkins illuminates the apparent and not so apparent choices that support pastors in yielding fruit for the long run. He helps us hear how these pastoral leaders made a positive and lasting impact on the faith lives of their congregations and communities. From his listening, he crafts their stories—stories of fruitful pastors, and more: confirmation of these fruitful ministries in the reflections of their congregational members.

"Fruit that lasts" is a central metaphor for this book. It is also an apt metaphor for the growing movement attending to "pastoral excellence," often planted through initiatives of the Lilly Endowment. Pastoral excellence is explicated by authors such as L. Gregory Jones and Kevin R. Armstrong in *Resurrecting Excellence*, Jackson W. Carroll in *God's Potters*, and Christian Scharen in *Faith as a Way of Life*. To use another biblical metaphor, these stories of fruitful pastoral leaders become for the reader a word made flesh. These pastors live out the excellence commended in theories and investigated in research. Their stories stand alongside those of their colleagues Lillian Daniel and Martin B. Copenhaver in *This Odd and Wondrous Calling*. They are the clergy counterpart of the healthy congregations Diana Butler Bass describes in *Christianity for the Rest of Us*.

Paul Hopkins is a pastoral leader whose own story forms a subtext to the book, another word made flesh. He too, has struggled with the question, "How can my ministry make a lasting difference?" He has endured seasons of profound discouragement and clinical depression. He has planted fruitful ministries in the church as well as in pastoral counseling. As the former executive director of the Samaritan Counseling Center in Albuquerque, New Mexico, Hopkins' leadership provides a breathing example of fruit that lasts.

I met Paul Hopkins when I was between two ministries—leaving my role as faculty and executive director and joining the national staff of the Samaritan Institute, directing its Clergy and Congregation Care project (also largely funded by the Lilly Endowment). He listened skillfully to me and my hope for Samaritan Centers to provide more resources for pastoral excellence. He encouraged me to become a midwife to Samaritan Centers, helping them envision and fashion resources for clergy and congregations grounded in the unique needs of their community. His wise counsel remains with me still, and will remain with the readers of this kind book as he encourages them to become grounded in their own unique and fruitful ministries.

This is a book for all pastoral leaders: those new to ministry and those who are near retirement. It is for women and men, for parish pastors and pastors who serve beyond the local congregation. These stories are not identical; as Hopkins writes, "none of them provides a universal model for effective ministry." Nor can they; what makes for effective ministry is as varied as the 365,000 pastors serving an estimated 350,000 congregations in the United States. Each story gives the reader a chance to identify with an effective pastor; each story an opportunity to listen for the resonance with their own ministry and congregation. Each story helps ministers find ways to reconnect to the vine that sustains fruitful ministry. These stories are nothing less than witness to the God who gives us life and calls us to ministry.

These stories are a word—a word about pastoral excellence—made flesh in the lives of seven pastoral leaders. Their impact expands as the reader takes in this word and embodies the word in his or her ministry. Here is Hopkins' invitation: read these stories with a small group of companions. Like the excellent listener that he is, Hopkins has written reflection and discussion questions for each chapter. What would happen if you, reader, gathered five to eight of your colleagues and formed a "circle of trust," as Parker Palmer describes those sacred groups of confidentiality where one can speak and be listened into wholeness? What if you and your colleagues read these stories, allowed the words to sink into your souls, and listened to the reverberations in your lives and ministries? What if you were able to discern and follow your calls into even deeper faithfulness? Then these stories would become a word made flesh beyond the pages of this book. As Hopkins writes, "this is your invitation—to define how that ancient story of God's transforming love is being renewed and deepened through your pastoral leadership, now and in the days to come."

God's transforming love sometimes seems a long distance from the world clergy inhabit: "the challenges facing both the church and the world in the early twenty-first century are daunting, and the climate for undertaking a life of pastoral leadership may be forbiddingly spare," writes Hopkins. In this book we receive a word about pastoral excellence that not only has much fruit to offer—this word reconnects pastoral leaders with the source of that fruitfulness, the love of God in Christ. It offers an opportunity to deepen our "pastoral imaginations,"as Craig Dykstra, vice president for religion at the Lilly Endowment writes, "a way of seeing the world through eyes of faith." For opportunities to renew and strengthen our call to God's ministry, we are grateful for this book, its stories of witness, and the wise listener who heard and wrote about fruit that lasts.

Nancy Gieseler Devor, M.Div., Ph.D.
Vice President, The Samaritan Institute
Director, Samaritan Institute Clergy and
    Congregation Care project

"Bear Fruit that Will Last"

Not long ago I was counseling with a fifty-eight-year-old, second-career pastor who was burning himself out and jeopardizing his marriage by working sixty to seventy hours a week in his pastoral-sized parish.[1] He was clinically depressed, ground down by his desperate quest to be faithful to the call to ministry about which he'd had such high hopes when he retired from his civil-service job and went off to seminary. "I had been thinking for years of bringing Christ's love to the lost and helping build the kingdom," Dave said woefully, "but the demands of this church are just more than I can keep up with. The work never ends, and I'm not sure what difference I'm really making in people's lives."

As a pastoral counselor, I have seen many Daves—and Sarahs and Manuels—over the past thirty-five years. Clergy have often come to talk with me in times of crisis, while others have come during the process of formation. Others have wisely sought to maintain or deepen wellness through support groups and retreats and the continuing-education events our counseling center has offered. Protestant and Roman Catholic, Orthodox and Anglican, men and women, English-speaking and Spanish-speaking, young and old have come to our counseling center from small and large congregations in rural and urban settings, seeking healing and guidance, consolation and companionship as they told their stories of pain and hope. Most often, they have been looking for direction to maintain or recapture the zeal they once felt, or for reassurance that their ministries might have significance. I share the longing of these pastors for ministry that matters, and I have known at times the discouragement and even despair some of them have expressed. Dark nights of the soul are very real—especially, I believe, for clergy.

I also remember being a twenty-three-year-old seminarian, debating with my fellow students the wisdom of channeling our boundless energy into lives of parish ministry. Of course, we debated the wisdom of almost everything in those days. It was the nature of the times, the seminary setting, and our youthful idealism. But even as we threw ourselves into the study of New Testament Greek and church administration, we asked ourselves, "Is leading a parish the best way to love God and serve the world?"

Most of us in those days served churches on weekends as student pastors, and so we were exposed to the real human needs met by parish ministers. I recall sitting in Dr. Schwartz's living room in Medford, Oklahoma, the evening after his death with his new widow and several neighbors and fellow congregants, listening to stories about his wonderful life as a small-town dentist. That night remains a treasured memory now, more than forty years later. (And I still feel twinges of embarrassment about spilling coffee on Dr. Schwartz's favorite brown recliner that evening in my nervousness at this, my first funeral preparation.) We also encountered the remarkable endurance and occasionally exasperating stubbornness of church life. The elders of that Medford congregation, for example, kept pining for more young people to join the church, but they consistently complained about the disruption of noisy children when two or three would show up on Sunday mornings.

We seminarians, bursting with enthusiasm for the gospel but already chastened by the realities of the very human churches we served, asked ourselves most often two questions: (1) Considering the many wonderful ways in which people might serve God, is ordained ministry the best way I can make a difference in the world? and (2) If my calling is truly to ordained ministry, how can I be sure that my work makes a lasting difference? This book assumes that the reader has answered the first question "Yes." It is written for those who have chosen ordained ministry as a way to answer God's call to serve and change the world. Like Richard, whose story we tell in chapter 2, we might resonate with the words of his college adviser, who suggested that politics and ministry were the two most effective paths to changing the world. But ministry, that adviser argued, is more significant because "there you are dealing with ultimate realities."

So we "surrendered to the call," as our Southern Baptist brothers (and a few sisters) might have put it, either recently or long ago. And now, looking both forward and back at some point on this path of ministry, we still ask ourselves: *How can my ministry make a lasting difference?* We believe, and we take seriously, the words of Jesus to his followers as described by John's Gospel: "You did not choose me but I chose you. And I appointed you to go and bear fruit, fruit that will last" (John 15:16). We can imagine ourselves in that upper room with the eleven remaining disciples and feel the joy of that blessing and the weight of that charge.

Like countless others who over the centuries have accepted this divine appointment, we acknowledge that planting and pruning and harvesting the fruit of the gospel is our work. And when we accept that call to serve, we recognize that inherent in the call is an expectation that we provide effective leadership that fosters enduring results. This book aims to help pastoral leaders make a lasting and positive difference in the lives of the people and communities they serve. The intention is that it will accomplish this goal by:

- Identifying characteristics and practices by which leadership endures beyond the season of the pastor's specific ministry.
- Encouraging and inspiring pastors to exercise pastoral leadership that continues to bear rich fruit in the lives of people, parishes, and communities.
- Describing disciplines that pastors may practice to tend their own vines so as to ensure lasting fruitfulness in their work.

The heart of this book is in the stories of seven pastors whose ministries exemplify ways of "bearing fruit that lasts." These are not famous pastors occupying historic pulpits but ordinary clergy whose pastoral leadership has become extraordinary. They could have been our fellow seminarians, all of whom answered the first question "yes" and since that time have taken various paths in response to the second question. While their stories are shared to highlight important characteristics that nurture fruitful pastoral leadership, they are also offered to invite readers to examine their own stories.

My own story has inevitably become intertwined with the stories in this book, so let me give you mine in a nutshell. A fourth-generation Disciples of Christ minister, I am the son of two ordained clergy. My mother was one of the first women ordained in my tradition, and my father's father was the leader of our denomination for a time. Ministry is in my blood. I was ordained in 1969 in Ponca City, Oklahoma, where Henry Warnsholz from that little Medford church I served as a student pastor placed his calloused farmer hands on my head alongside the hands of several other pastors and teachers and fellow seminarians, blessing me for ministry.

Since that time I have worked in congregational, regional, and national levels of the church, giving particular attention to clergy leadership. As a pastoral counselor and educator, I have worked closely with pastors and churches from many parishes and denominations, providing counseling for clergy in distress, candidacy assessment for those sensing a call to ordination, education for pastors in formation, and consultation to congregations and judicatories to strengthen and sustain effective pastoral leaders. For three years I served as director of education for the Missouri School of Religion, working primarily in training and supporting pastors of small and rural parishes, and during that time I served as an adjunct faculty member of Eden Theological Seminary in St. Louis. As I finish writing this book, I have just completed eighteen years as CEO of a pastoral-counseling center, where I led that organization's healing ministry and oversaw a "Sustaining Pastoral Excellence" project, funded by the Lilly Endowment, serving clergy and congregations in the Southwest.

Celebrating the fortieth anniversary of one's ordination and moving into retirement from a demanding ministry of pastoral leadership brings a special poignancy to the question of lasting fruitfulness. I have lunch periodically with a group of other men who are nearing retirement (my OGR group—Old Guys Retiring), and all of us in our various careers ask this question in a variety of ways: Will my work continue to make a difference in the lives of individuals and institutions and even the surrounding world? I hope that by wrestling with this question early in a career—or at the five- to ten-year mark of ministry, when research has shown that discouragement may become most profound—the reader will think not only about the value of longevity in ministry, but even more about ways to enhance the enduring impact of pastoral leadership.

No book, of course, is by itself going to save ministers from the sort of misguided mission that was driving Dave, the pastor I mentioned earlier. But I do wish for him a book that he might read and discuss with colleagues, one that will help him rediscover the joy of his calling as well as guard against its seductions, and even inspire him to exercise his pastoral leadership with new wisdom and good stewardship. I wish for him not the ephemeral productivity of activity that at times becomes frantic, as he seems to think is necessary, but the rich gracefulness of fecundity, as Henri Nouwen called it in his book *Lifesigns*.[2] Such grace comes only from a deep awareness that he did not choose God, but that God chose him to bear fruit that lasts.

I think Dave, and also you, the reader, would profit most from this book by reading it together with a small group of companions as you journey along the sometimes arduous, sometimes joyous path of ministry. You might read a chapter a week and then gather to discuss your reactions, share ideas, and encourage one another in your work. I've provided some questions to prompt your discussion, but you may choose to discard those and focus on your own questions and thoughts. That's the kind of self-directed resourcefulness that John Wimmer of the Lilly Endowment has, through countless research projects across the country, found to be necessary for fruitful ministry. And as you read and discuss, be always mindful of the high significance of your call. Your vocation grants you the privilege of participating in God's transformation of human lives—including your own! God bless you as you toil to "bear fruit that lasts."

Gratitude

I've been fortunate to have enjoyed in my life rich opportunities for satisfying ministry and wonderful companions along the way. Best of all, my ministry has been graced by eloquent teachers and wise mentors who have shown me how to be a fruitful pastoral leader. Some of those have been especially important to me in writing this book.

- Bill and Paul and Rod and Jim, pastors whose extraordinary leadership I have admired and whose friendship I cherish.
- Joel and David and Curtis, spiritual directors who taught me about God's generous providence and who have kept me faithful.
- LaDonna, my wife, who taught me almost everything I know about hospitality, forgiveness, and love, and who taught a community about giving abundantly.
- Sarah, whose firm leadership, honest feedback, and respectful companionship for fifteen years made it possible for me to be a good leader.
- Beth, whose collegiality, wit, and editorial wisdom made this book possible—and far better than I could have imagined.
- Sherman, whose generous life and friendship have led our city to be a more charitable place.
- Bob and Fred and Frank and Russell, whose pastoral leadership is still bearing fruit that lasts in me.
- Richard and Russell and Christine and Trey and Carole and Sue and Paul, who shared their stories so openly with me. By God's grace they have transformed their small corners of the world, and have borne fruit that lasts.

Thank you!

chapter 1

Call to Fruitful Leadership

I n her Pulitzer Prize–winning biography of the Rev. Henry Ward Beecher,[1] historian Debby Applegate tells the story of how Beecher became, during the middle of the nineteenth century, deserving of Abraham Lincoln's claim that he was "the most influential man in America." His passionate preaching against slavery made him a champion of the abolition movement, and in the fight for racial justice, he was a forerunner to an even more famous clergyman of recent times, the Rev. Dr. Martin Luther King Jr. The son of a "fire-and-brimstone" preacher who early in life appeared unpromising compared to his more talented siblings, Henry Ward Beecher spent most of his career as a parish pastor preaching a gospel of unconditional love. His most enduring pastoral labors built Brooklyn's Plymouth Congregational Church into one of the country's most dynamic congregations. And although his later years were tainted by allegations of infidelity with a parishioner, his leadership was undeniably a powerful ecclesiastical and cultural force that changed people's lives and paved the way for modern American Christianity.

Pastoral leaders, whether saintly or even deeply flawed, have transformed the world in sometimes visible, and much more often quiet ways for two thousand years. But as Daniel Aleshire,

1

executive director of the Association of Theological Schools has pointed out, the central role of church leaders in shaping culture and intellectual life in colonial America has gradually diminished over the years.[2] Few pastoral leaders now exercise the kind of influence that Beecher and King exerted, and not many possess the oratorical gifts that contributed to their fame. While Rick Warren, T. D. Jakes, Bill Hybels, and a handful of others attract some national attention from their pulpits, the vast majority of the 365,000 clergy serving an estimated 350,000 congregations in the United States today serve humbly within their own communities with little public notice. And since the average size of all U.S. congregations is now about seventy-five participating members, clergy are rarely even in a position to have much impact on their own communities.[3]

But Christian leaders do change lives. What's more, the church's leaders, many from their posts as parish pastors, have exercised pastoral, priestly, and prophetic ministries that have changed history. The contributions of these saints have been recognized in many ways, rarely more evocatively than in the litany that is chanted annually during the All Saint's Day Eucharist at the Church of St. Stephen and the Incarnation in Washington, D.C. The following excerpts from that litany illustrate the rich diversity of leaders who have advanced our faith:

> Thomas the doubter; Augustine of Canterbury; Francis Xavier; Samuel Joseph Schereschewsky; all travelers who carried the Gospel to distant places . . .
>
> Bernard and Dominic; Catherine of Siena, the scourge of popes; John and Charles Wesley, preachers in the streets; all whose power of speaking gave life to the written word . . .
>
> Benedict of Nursia; Teresa of Avila; Nicholas Ferrar; Elizabeth Ann Seton; Richard Meux Benson; Charles de Foucauld; all founders of communities . . .
>
> Amos of Tekoa, who held up the plumbline; John Wycliffe, who brought the Scripture to the common folk; John Hus and Menno Simons, generals in the Lamb's war; Martin Luther, who could do no other; George Fox, foe of steeple-houses; all who kept the Church ever-reforming . . .

> Paul the apostle, transfixed by noonday light; Augustine of Hippo, God's city planner; Thomas Aquinas and John Calvin, architects of the divine; Charles Williams, teacher of coinherence; Karl Barth, knower of the unknowable; all who saw God at work and wrote down what they saw . . .[4]

The ranks of these famous leaders are vastly expanded, however, by the countless ministers who have faithfully served congregations of Christians through the centuries and around the world. The leadership pastors offer to individuals, churches, and the world is vital to the enduring fruitfulness of Christ's ongoing work of redemption on earth. Their most essential work builds and sustains nothing less than the living body of Jesus Christ. They accompany believers through life's important passages, both painful and joyous, and celebrate sacraments that affirm the reality of divine grace in our midst. They teach the faith, and they prophesy about the demands of that faith in the larger world; sometimes they are even on the front lines in translating those demands into concrete action. Pastors are, quite simply, God's hands in shaping the church and even all creation. The fields these quiet servants have planted and tended have produced a rich harvest that has lasted through the centuries.

But the demands and circumstances of modern ministry are different now. The theological education of most current American church ministers has emphasized a combination of intellectual rigor and practical skills that may now be proving inadequate to the changing nature of the contemporary church. Brian McLaren, prophet of the emerging church movement, points out, "Instead of implementing someone else's preexisting formula (i.e., orthodoxy or denominational doctrine), you now have to help a community come to some sort of cohesion. . . . So the strengths needed are community building and organization more than institutional management."[5] McLaren's analysis points contemporary religious leaders to the need for adaptive leadership, like that described by Ronald Heifetz at Harvard's Center for Public Leadership in his book *Leadership Without Easy Answers*,[6] which goes beyond short-term technical solutions to genuinely transformative change.

Pressing challenges

Serving as a pastoral leader continues to offer rich opportunity for those who are willing to undertake its rigors. Pursuing a life dedicated to lofty spiritual ideals and focused on building organizational effectiveness in a church while healing a terribly broken world is a pearl of great price. But the challenges facing both the church and the world in the early twenty-first century are daunting, and the climate for undertaking a life of pastoral leadership may be forbiddingly spare, often lacking in worldly comforts and satisfactions.

Fewer young people, in fact, are choosing a life of professional ministry these days. Enrollment in seminaries affiliated with the Association of Theological Schools has been steadily declining since 2005, and the average age of students is increasing. The Barna Research Group points out that the median age of a mainline senior pastor just ten years ago was forty-eight; today it's fifty-five.[7] One reason for this decline in young people pursuing ministry may be that a pastor's life is much more stressful now than it was even a generation ago.

Financial stress is certainly one area that significantly affects ministerial satisfaction. Clergy salaries have barely kept up with inflation and compare unfavorably with compensation in many other sectors of society. What's more, a growing number of pastors are coming out of seminary with burdensome debt, and the dwindling number of churches that can pay a living wage means that new pastors' options for erasing that debt are diminishing. The Rev. Joyce Lieberman, associate for call system support for the Presbyterian Church U.S.A., points out that 50 percent of Presbyterian congregations have fewer than one hundred members, but only 9 percent of ministers searching for churches are willing to go to those small churches, largely for financial reasons.[8] Meanwhile, the numbers of bi-vocational and non-seminary-trained ministers are increasing, and these pastors often must cope with the demands of balancing two jobs while doing this important work with insufficient training.

Family financial limitations are not the only stressors. Married clergy, like most married Americans, are much more often part of two-career families these days, and the emotional and practical support of a nonemployed spouse that used to make ministry easier and even more rewarding is now unavailable to most ministers. Congregations' expectations that their pastors stem the tide of decline and replace it with increasing numbers of new members may place impossible burdens on clergy performance. Publicity about clerical misconduct has undermined confidence in clergy as community role models, making the pastoral life more difficult and reducing for some their trust in their own calling. Diminishing denominational resources, furthermore, lead to fewer institutional support systems for clergy.

The systems within which clergy work foster expectations that ministers be producers—of stimulating sermons, successful programs, more congregants, and increasing dollars. The pressures from congregational and denominational leaders for pastors to be productive emphasize measurable results, often to the detriment of self-care, spiritual nurture, and the immeasurable gift of genuine Christian community. Most of those who enter ministry do so for altruistic reasons, but the requirements of a balanced church budget and awareness of comparative salary lists often prompt clergy dissatisfaction. As a result, spiritual values may become overshadowed by secular standards of success and reward. Secular measures are important, of course, just as secular resources can be incorporated into the practice of pastoral leadership. Still, excellence in ministry would certainly be bolstered by higher compensation, better training, shorter workweeks, more secure health and retirement plans, healthier congregations, and higher esteem in the culture. But the church's pursuit of these assets for its clergy has yielded lackluster results.

Internally, too many of today's pastors have become barren and dry. In a desperate quest to fulfill the demands of the world, clergy can be lured into the error of Aaron, constructing golden calves instead of patiently awaiting word from the mountain, or going there themselves. Well-crafted public prayer has too often become a substitute for vital personal prayer. Sabbath rest may be supplanted by car pools to children's soccer games and efforts to catch up with paperwork. Devotional reading is transformed into pragmatic sermon preparation. Spiritual growth is measured by continuing-education credits. In my own work as a pastoral counselor, I have seen far too many clergy whose spiritual desolation has led to ineffectiveness rooted in despair or clinical depression. Sometimes that dryness has prompted misconduct or an escape from ministry in pursuit of a more rewarding life.

While pastors are facing difficult vocational challenges in a rapidly changing church milieu, the mission of the church to heal and serve the world remains paramount—and that world faces profound difficulties. Global terrorism has heightened suspicion and misunderstanding among the world's peoples, and those who would cynically exploit the consequent anxieties for political gain have fanned the flames of distrust and fear. At the same time, a global recession born of widespread greed and inadequate restraints has eroded the well-being of the poor and the middle class while weakening the safety nets upon which the poor have relied—including the church. Our ability as a nation to address problems effectively has diminished as talk radio and political partisanship have become more bitter, and the effects of this trend on civil discourse among people of faith has been tragic. Meanwhile, the well-being of our created world is jeopardized by rampant consumerism and overreliance on fossil fuels. Consensus about how to address these environmental problems, which threaten our very existence, is elusive. The list of the world's critical problems is incredibly long, and it is not our purpose here to define exhaustively the world's great needs that our own hearts' longings might address (with appreciation for Presbyterian author Frederick Buechner's definition of vocation as the place where these two intersect[9]). For our purposes, it is sufficient to say that the world offers countless opportunities for salvific Christian ministries of justice and care. Pastoral leadership can and should be nothing less than a fundamental resource in healing and saving the world.

Varieties of gifts

How to carry out that important leadership, however, is not so clear. Human diversity and the wide range of theological and ecclesiastical expressions of the ministry of Jesus Christ foster an incredibly rich spectrum of strategies and tactics for the exercise of pastoral leadership. What's more, the demands of pastoral leadership in what some have called this "post-Christian" age have become more complicated, regardless of traditional ecclesiastical expectations and constraints. Biblical models sometimes offer useful instruction. Furthermore, leadership theories developed in business and education and psychology have added further possibilities for refinement and application of historic ecclesiastical guidelines. There is not just one way to be a pastoral leader—and certainly not just a single right way!

In his letters to the early church, the apostle Paul recognized many possible ways of performing ministry. In those early days, of course, there was no separate class of leaders called clergy. But Paul understood the importance of the various talents people brought to leadership. It was not just the apostles who led the church, but people with "varieties of gifts": uttering wisdom; speaking knowledge; healing; working miracles; prophesying; speaking in tongues and interpreting tongues; teaching; exhorting; giving; leading; showing compassion; doing evangelism; being pastors. (See 1 Corinthians 12; Romans 12; Ephesians 4.) Some of these possibilities were definite roles in the church that over time became formalized as specialized ministries. Others were broader characteristics of personality and behavior that served the community and advanced the gospel.

The biblical record identifies many roles and characteristics for faith community leaders. Moses is called, in a mystical encounter with a burning bush, to lead the people of Israel out of bondage despite his shadowy past and his faulty oratory. Aaron is called to be Moses's associate and sometimes spokesman. Jethro, Moses's father-in-law, points out that his congregation is too large to give everyone individual attention and suggests that Moses appoint assistants to do some of the work. Ruth recognizes the importance of following her mother-in-law into a new life for herself and her descendents. Esther, having been named queen of Persia, becomes an advocate who saves her people from annihilation. Prophets like Jeremiah and Amos and Hosea are called to speak hard truths to the people. John the Baptist undertakes a life of deprivation to herald the coming of Jesus. Jesus models the importance of effective teaching and healing, emphasizing by example that the best way to lead is by being a servant. Various women who were followers of Jesus, named and unnamed by the patriarchal writers of the day, provide practical help to Jesus's ministry and become the first proclaimers of his resurrection, although they are sadly dismissed as unreliable. Paul and his various associates and assistants become evangelists, spreading the gospel throughout the Mediterranean region. Deacons are appointed to serve the tangible needs of the growing community of faith. These saints, and many others throughout church history, have offered rich models for countless preachers and pastoral leaders.

Now, in this age of scientific rigor, models and metaphors for effective leadership in both the church and the world have been tested and propagated even more widely. Secular books and articles about leadership, academic degree programs, and continuing-education seminars are attracting the attention of religious leaders and institutions, and emerging theories of leadership are being tried out in congregational settings and discussed among ministers. We'll see some of the useful and creative ways these leadership theories and practices are being applied in ministry through the stories of pastors told later in this book. The quest to define excellence in pastoral leadership is well underway.

Many of the leadership theories attracting interest among pastors today are *person-centered*, focusing on the personality, values, and actions of the leader. Robert Greenleaf's classic volume, *Servant Leadership*,[10] was an early example of this approach, and it has spawned a nationwide movement among religious, nonprofit, and business leaders, resourced largely by the Greenleaf Center for Servant Leadership in Indianapolis. Psychologist Daniel Goleman has compellingly reframed the way we think about human intelligence to focus on the central role of emotional and interpersonal sensitivity, and then with his colleagues has applied these discoveries to the nature of good leaders in their book *Primal Leadership*.[11] Finally, Jim Collins conducted rigorous research distinguishing great companies from merely good ones in his widely referenced *Good to Great*[12] and has determined that leaders of these great companies, whom he called "Level 5 Leaders," displayed "a paradoxical mix of personal humility and professional will."

In the religious world, pastor and author N. Graham Standish has built upon this rich resource of personal leadership theories with his recent book *Humble Leadership*,[13] inviting pastors to undergird a servant approach with confident trust in God's guidance and grace. Alban Institute consultant Roy Oswald, writing with colleague Otto Kroeger, wrote an immensely helpful book on pastoral leadership, *Personality Type and Religious Leadership*,[14] that applies the widely used Myers-Briggs Type Indicator (MBTI) to the practical work of ministry. Parker Palmer, an educator with deep spiritual roots, has convincingly proclaimed in his book *A Hidden Wholeness*[15] the importance of living "an undivided life," and his writings and workshops have offered guidance to many religious leaders as they seek to lead lively communities of faith. More recently, building on teachings of narrative psychology, writers such as Richard Hester and Kelli Walker-Jones, in their book *Know Your Story and Lead with It*,[16] have affirmed the importance to leaders of understanding the impact of their own life stories as they guide the life and work of churches.

Other writers have emphasized *systemic* approaches to leadership, underscoring the necessity of understanding and practicing leadership within the organizational context. The late Rabbi Edwin Friedman was one of the first proponents of this approach within religious circles and certainly has become the most widely known. Building upon the family systems theory of psychologist Murray Bowen, Friedman's hallmark emphases in his book *Generation to Generation*[17] on "defining self and staying in touch" and "managing the anxiety in the system" by being "self-differentiated" have guided countless pastoral leaders toward more effective ministries. Church consultant Peter Steinke has extended Friedman's theories in several ways, applying a rich trove of congregational experience to his writings, most notably in his book *Congregational Leadership in Anxious Times*.[18] Management consultant and teacher Margaret Wheatley has drawn upon the world of physics and chemistry to interpret the tasks of leadership in the living organisms we call organizations, writing most compellingly in her book *Leadership and the New Science*.[19] Out of the emerging church world, Kansas City pastor Tim Keel, in his book *Intuitive Leadership*,[20] has combined a systemic approach with a central emphasis on the role of narrative in shaping and leading dynamic churches.

A third group of theories, which I will call *functional*, is best represented by Max De Pree, Stephen Covey, and the team of James Kouzes and Barry Posner. These writers have documented, and especially in Covey's case named in memorable ways, various strategies and tactics for effecting change in individual lives of leaders and the corporate life of organizations. Max De Pree's little volume *Leadership Is an Art* draws primarily upon the author's experience and observations as an industrial CEO and conveys in simple but compelling fashion how effective leaders operate, beginning with this observation: "The first responsibility of a leader is to define reality. The last is to say thank you."[21] Covey, of course, is the originator of the widely popular "7 Habits" series of books. His best-selling first volume, *The 7 Habits of Highly Effective People*,[22] introduced readers to what he called seven habits—be proactive; begin with the end in mind; put first things first; think win/win; seek first to understand, then to be understood; synergize; and sharpen the saw. These terms have become guideposts for countless leaders in business, church, and community. Kouzes and Posner, business professors at Santa Clara University, have written and lectured widely on what they call "five practices of exemplary leadership": model the way; inspire a shared vision; challenge the process; enable others to act; and encourage the heart. They have also brought particular focus to the implications of their theory for the Christian community in editing their book *Christian Reflections on the Leadership Challenge*.[23]

Finally, there is a more complex theory I will call *transformational* leadership. The importance of change is, of course, considered within all of these theories of leadership. In fact, there is considerable overlap among them, and the distinctions among the categories I have offered here are not as neat as I might wish. But in all these theories, truly transformational change is seldom addressed adequately. Ronald Heifetz, founder of the Center for Public Leadership at Harvard's John F. Kennedy School of Government, is the most articulate analyst of such radical reform. Calling his approach "adaptive leadership," Heifetz argues that we must go beyond consideration of the personality or activities of the leader to examine core values and beliefs while also addressing the system's internal conflicts.[24] Adaptive leadership acknowledges the significance of systems and functions, but it advocates reaching beyond a short-term focus on solving immediate technical problems. The real goal of adaptive leadership is to help organizations attain a new level of effectiveness by collectively engaging people in owning and working at deeper solutions to the challenges they are facing.

Heifetz speaks primarily out of academia with broad experience honed in the worlds of public policy and commercial enterprise, but his vision is strangely familiar to those of us informed by the Christian story. His call for "adaptive change" is not at all unlike Jesus's call for fresh wineskins to carry the new wine of God's transforming love. The Christian story, while occasionally bogging down in addressing what Heifetz would call short-term technical problems, offers an inspiring vision of radical change. It is always founded upon God's love, and it is always lived out most fully as people respond to that divine love with a love of their own. The gathered community of those aspiring lovers that we call the church is called to interpret and embody that love within its own life and in its engagement with the world. So when Jesus says to his disciples that they must love one another as he has loved them, then goes on to say that he chose them to "go and bear fruit, fruit that will last" (John 15:16), he has something very specific in mind. He is directing those who will carry on his work to devote themselves to changing lives in a way that fosters enduring love. Effective pastoral leaders today will likely draw upon a wealth of leadership theories, strategies, and tactics, such as those I have briefly described here. The fundamental focus of the work of pastoral leaders, their fruit, must be transforming the lives of people, churches, and the world.

NOW THEY OWN THE VISION

"The difference between leaving a legacy and having provided lasting leadership is that it's not about me. It's about the church." Jim's thoughts about leadership that has lasting

effects come from many years of parish ministry and experience as a judicatory official. He had left St. John's Church several years earlier, and looking back, he's pleased to see some
of the programs he launched, like the children's worship program or the interfaith ministry to homeless families, continuing to make a difference in people's lives. But he thinks the
most lasting effect of his leadership at St. John's was his work
in helping the church's members identify who they are and
where they are going. "They cast a vision for themselves, and
now they own it, and it endures."

Fruitful leadership

Pastors and theologians have talked about this call to loving transformation in many ways. Henri Nouwen, in his little book *Lifesigns*, framed it evocatively in terms of fruitfulness. As a Catholic
priest, Nouwen saw clearly how Christians could be drawn into
a works-orientation that emphasizes productivity and loses sight
of the more radical vision of fecundity that he believes Jesus had
in mind. In words that surely ring true for many contemporary
pastors, Nouwen suggested that productivity is often driven by a
fearful quest to prove one's worth instead of a graceful response
to divine love. He does not dismiss the value of productivity, acknowledging that production is sometimes necessary to our lives
and work. He does, however, insist that we always remember that
ours is a higher calling: "But when our value as human beings
depends on what we make with our hands and minds, we become
victims of the fear tactics of our world."[25]

Nouwen's words make me think about my friend Clyde. When
he was senior pastor of a downtown United Methodist church,
Clyde agonized about the statistical report he was required to
submit to his district superintendent each year, documenting baptisms, new members, records of giving, and fulfillment of expected
financial support to the broader church. "The effectiveness of my
ministry gets reduced to a set of numbers," he moaned, "and if
I don't produce, I'll find myself appointed to a smaller parish."

United Methodists do not have a corner on demands for account-ability, of course. Annual reports to the denomination come in many forms, and nondenominational pastors deal with similar du-ties and comparisons. (As one pastor put it, "I'm evaluated on two things: bodies and bucks.")[26] In the clergy support groups we sponsor in our counseling center, we've learned to limit member-ship to one person from each tradition in a group, because so many pastors have told us that denominational groupings lead inevitably to informal contests about whose numbers are better or to silent shame about declining numbers. The pressure to be productive from the broader church, and often from within the pastor's own mind, is ever present.

In contrast to Clyde's experience, retired professor of homilet-ics Fred Craddock suggests a different vision of fruitfulness. Fred told me a story about a friend of his who wanted Craddock to go with him to hear "the greatest preacher in Atlanta." Fred went and heard a sermon that was "not very good, really," but he quickly understood that his friend valued this man's preaching because the preacher had conducted a couple of funerals for members of this man's family, had performed a wedding for another member, and had been a pastor to the family on many occasions. Despite having devoted his life to teaching the art of good preaching, and being named by one survey as one of America's top ten preachers himself, Craddock has always understood that the real impact of ministry is to be found in relationships. He observed:

> Just preaching about things, and using big words like *salvation* and *re-demption*, is not enough. We have to go to floor level and be one of them. The good pastor must be willing to risk who he is in order to understand who they are. It goes back to the word *person*, or *parson*, to describe this minister.[27]

So how are we to measure fecundity without losing our humanity and succumbing to the false god of productivity? In my own field of pastoral counseling, we are increasingly subject to constraints imposed by managed care, including expectations for measur-able outcomes. Evidence-based therapies are in vogue, witnessing to the health-care system's growing demand for convincing data about the value of treatment and its cost-effectiveness. But in the church (and in the specialized field of pastoral counseling, I might add), being midwife to new life and nurturing vital community are often more craft than science, and hard to measure.

A recent trend, spurred largely by the Lilly Endowment's "Sustaining Pastoral Excellence" initiative, has focused on defining and encouraging excellence as a standard for pastoral leadership. L. Gregory Jones and Kevin Armstrong have helpfully captured ideas emanating from the Duke Divinity School's Colloquium on Excellence in Ministry. In their scholarly book *Resurrecting Excellence*,[28] they frame a vision of excellence in ministry through the three images of calling, profession, and office, and they reflect upon the importance of the related gifts of attentiveness, practical wisdom, and administration as facets of such excellence. The authors go on to suggest that excellence can best be cultivated by drawing upon what Craig Dykstra, vice-president for religion at Lilly Endowment, has wonderfully called "pastoral imagination." Pastoral imagination, Dykstra says, lovingly encounters the hard reality of the parish and the people within it and looks for creative ways to do practical ministry in community that witnesses to and extends God's reign.[29] His is, I think, another way of talking about adaptive leadership applied to the specific context of pastoral leadership.

Jackson Carroll, professor emeritus at Duke Divinity School, warns against the seductions of excellence as a model for fruitful ministry. He notes that the contemporary quest for excellence in American culture has emerged from the world of business, where economic success is most highly prized. He points out that the values of the gospel, which celebrate the poor and the outcast more than the rich and powerful, and which lift up the sacrifice of the cross as a path to triumph, may not be compatible with this secular ideal of excellence. Nevertheless, Carroll does identify five "marks of excellent ministry" that he believes are congruent with and may support excellence in the pastoral context. These marks are resiliency and the practice of spiritual disciplines; agility and reflective leadership; trust and personal authority; the practice of staying connected; and self-directed, career-long learn-ing.[30] We will see elements of these "marks of excellence" often in the stories of pastoral leadership told in the following chapters of this book.

What, then, are the fruits that spring from such excellence in pastoral leadership? Numbers of baptisms, pastoral visits, funer-als and weddings conducted, and dollars given to the church—these will always be factors in assessing the results of contempo-rary American ministry. The church-growth movement in recent times has sometimes elevated the attraction of new members to nearly idolatrous centrality, although the social-justice wing of the church might also be found guilty of its own prideful emphases, particularly when growth in numbers is dismissed as insignificant compared to the pursuit of justice. As Henri Nouwen has con-ceded, producing results is not a bad thing, even when the results are numerical. Jesus's parables of the sower and of the talents, to name just two, specifically lift up numerical results as part of the benefit of sowing seeds. But the measure of fruitful ministry must go deeper than this.

Out of the agrarian culture in which he lived, Jesus talked quite a lot about bearing good fruit, and the image of fruitfulness is a rich one throughout the New Testament. Paul, in his letter to the church in Galatia, talked about the fruit of the Spirit as "love, joy, peace, patience, kindness, generosity, faithfulness, gentleness, and self-control" (Gal. 5:22–23). Such qualities are nearly impossible to measure with any precision, though their presence makes an enormous difference in the quality of life in the church and the world. When these fruits abound, lives are sweeter.

Jesus's farewell words to his disciples recorded in the Gospel of John may contain both the most comprehensive and the sim-plest description of the call to fruitfulness in pastoral leadership. In John 15 Jesus says three important things about fruitfulness that offer guidance to pastoral leaders in their work. First, Jesus is the central vine who connects God, the author of all life, with the branches, whose function is to bear fruit. So if pastoral lead-ers are to be fruitful, they must stay connected to God in Christ, the source of all fruitfulness. Those who lose that connection will wither and eventually be consigned to the fire (sounds like burnout to me!). Second, we do not choose to connect with the vine, but Christ chooses us, and makes us his friends. We must, of course, continue to say yes to that connection, and we must nurture that connection with spiritual discipline. But the initiative rests with Christ, and we are the responders. The fruitfulness of ministry is never just our doing. And finally, the essential fruit we are called to bear is love. As we have been loved by God in Christ, so our work must be to bear that love for others and to foster that love in them.

The fruits produced in love by excellent pastoral leadership are these: churches are healthier; people grow in faith; the world is healed. Healthy churches, like all healthy systems, are more resilient, are more likely to grow because of their openness and flexibility, and are more prone to look beyond their own internal concerns to the needs of the world they are called to serve. The story of Christine's church, told in chapter 4, is one example of a church growing healthier as a result of pastoral leadership. People who are growing in faith live their beliefs with greater devotion and more inquisitiveness about the meaning of those beliefs for their daily lives. Sue's pastoral leadership, described in chapter 7, has led many churches and clergy to such growth in faith. Healing of the world comes when people take faith's mandates of love and justice so seriously that they are compelled to enact those teachings in their communities. Trey's ministry, described in chapter 5, has generated such fruit in his congregation's work for social justice.

And what is it that makes this fruit lasting? "Fruit that will last" comes from plants with deep roots in rich soil. Such plants require thoughtful and disciplined attention patiently extended over time. Health comes not by pulling a weed or trimming a stray limb here and there. Lasting fruitfulness requires more than occasional brief interventions. Pastoral leaders who practice adaptive change are more likely to move people and churches beyond short-term technical solutions that simply offer transient stability. Their aim is enduring second-order change—change that brings a new and irreversible way of seeing things. Then the fruit itself becomes fruitful. Fruits have seeds, and as David McAllister-Wilson, president of Wesley Theological Seminary, has said, "To be a fruitful leader is to be an agent of God's future."[31]

Wineskins and baskets

Fruitful pastoral leaders, rather than adding a few lines or even a new chapter to a church's story, are more likely to help craft an entirely new story. Revelation's heavenly vision of "making all things new" is made real in transformed lives, enlivened congregations, and reformed structures of the world. Changes may be small or grand, but change must come. And stories told about the change become part of the change process itself.

Jesus was a storyteller. Yes, he gave sermons that described concepts and interpreted history and theology. And he made lists, like the beatitudes, that have offered guidance for Christian conduct for two thousand years. But his most powerful utterances, I think, were the parables he told—"Listen, a sower went out to sow. . ." These cogent stories offered glimpses of the kingdom he proclaimed. They were evocative and inductive, inviting his listeners to think about the meaning of his words for their lives. His listeners didn't always get it: "Seeing they do not perceive, and hearing they do not listen, nor do they understand" (Matt. 13:13). And sometimes he may have even gone on to explain the meaning of his stories in almost pedantic fashion, as he is reported to have done with this parable of the sower in Matthew 13.

Parables, for Jesus, were the containers within which could be found the full and practical meaning of the good news of God. Stories, in fact, have always been the principal means by which people have retained and conveyed and interpreted the meaning of their lives. History is fundamentally a collection of stories. The primary record of our faith's history, the Bible, is mostly a wonderful storybook composed of smaller stories that convey and explain the grand narrative of God's love for his people, along with his people's attempts to accept, understand, and live in the light of that divine love. And, as Fred Craddock would be quick to add, the best preaching not only grows out of the pastor's relationship with his or her people as well as their relationship to this grand narrative; it also conveys its wisdom best through storytelling. "The relationship gives authority to the voice," Craddock says, "and it must sustain a conversation among the people."[32] Through such conversations about the Christian story, the story itself is extended and even transformed.

What follows is mostly a collection of stories. I see these stories of pastoral leadership as wineskins and baskets that contain "fruit that will last." The seven pastors whose stories are briefly told are not perfect pastors. They are not saints any more than we all are "the saints" of whom the apostle Paul spoke so often. Their ministries are not famous, and they might not meet the world's criteria for success. But I believe their leadership has helped to transform ordinary people and ordinary churches in extraordinary ways. They have been fruitful, and the enduring fruit they have produced will help transform the world.

Following the seven stories, I will identify core characteristics that appear throughout these stories—pathways to leadership that lasts—which I believe contribute to the fruitfulness these pastors are bringing to the church. In the final chapter I'll look at some ways in which the church, and pastors themselves, might tend the vineyard, identifying ways in which bountiful ministries might be nurtured and sustained.

Just reading these stories and my analysis is not enough, however. Certainly there can be value in learning about pastors who at least one person thinks have provided leadership that is lasting. But there is infinitely more value in examining these stories together with a group of your peers. Just as Jesus told parables to invite his leaders to think about the meaning of those stories for them, so too I tell you these stories in hopes that you and your colleagues will find your own meanings in them. How are you being called to be fruitful? What are the fruits of your ministry that will last? What kind of leadership can and do you provide that creates "fruit that will last"? This is your invitation—to define how that ancient story of God's transforming love is being renewed and deepened through *your* pastoral leadership, now and in the days to come.

chapter 2

Pastoral Integrity

• *Richard* •

W hen the newly appointed archbishop began to clean up after the scandal of pedophile priests and his predecessor's disgraceful boundary violations, he called Richard in to be his new chancellor—the "chief operating officer" for the archdiocese. Helping the archdiocese recover from "Chernobyl on the Rio Grande," as the archbishop calls it, would require an extraordinary blend of pastoral sensitivity, deep spirituality, and delicate diplomacy. More than anything else, though, the job would require unquestioned personal integrity. After all, more than twenty priests had to be removed from their posts, countless victims had to be consoled, and even the former archbishop's sexual indiscretions had to be addressed. The reputation and indeed the effectiveness of the entire church's ministry was severely wounded. Richard, a quiet, widely respected priest in the archdiocese for twenty-five years, was just the man for the job.

Looking back on those dark days more than fifteen years ago, Richard shakes his head sadly. "Selfish interests have hurt us," he says of his beloved church, "but I hope we have begun to relearn that we must do what's best for the people, not just us." Spending seven years with lawyers was excruciating, he recalls, "but the evil of abuse had been shoved under the rug too long, and at last the church was forced to admit its sin. We are a stronger church and society now because we went through that difficult period."

He is right. In an archdiocese where once shame and anger prevailed, parishes are growing and vocations are increasing. New churches are being built. The archbishop credits Richard with being a significant sower of this new life, citing in particular his pastoral judgment, which "embodies compassion for the people and builds bridges rather than tearing them down. He brought the church forward to restore its health."

Now pastor of Risen Savior Catholic Community, a thriving parish of thirty-two hundred families in an upper-middle-class part of the city, Richard is a cherished and respected man of God. Yet even this particular ministry was born in grief, as Richard was called in to follow the church's beloved founding pastor, who had been forced to resign amid rumors of misconduct. Some parishioners resented Richard at first, seeing him as a sign of the archbishop's meddling in their parish. But Richard threw himself into his work, claimed his identity as an ordinary pastor, and began getting to know and to love the people. Kenn, his deacon colleague in ministry, says Richard took the stance, "I am who I am"—the epitome of pastoral self-differentiation (though I think Kenn probably meant the term more in the Popeye sense than the Yahweh sense). And now, ten years later, Kenn says most of those who left have come back, and thirty to forty new families are joining each month. The church's facilities have been expanded, and a fundamental climate of charity has been restored. Risen Savior is a healthy, growing church with a passion for mission, particularly to the poor.

Richard greeted me warmly when we met for lunch one spring day, just four blocks from his parish. His lanky frame displays the graceful athlete he has been all his life, and his smile suggests the playful spirit I saw the first time I visited his office at the parish. On the table by his desk he had proudly displayed a birthday card showing a couple driving an amusement-park bumper car, beneath which was the Ogden Nash quote: "You are only young once, but you can stay immature indefinitely." Sister Eva, who has known him in the archdiocese for many years, confirmed this self-deprecating image by sharing a story Richard tells about himself in his first parish. He began making sick calls in this small community's hospital and dutifully visited all the patients with "Cath" after their names in the charts, intending to offer them prayer and sacraments. After several rebuffs, he brought his puzzlement to a nurse who was a member of his parish, and she explained that "Cath" was an abbreviation for "catheter." Richard still does not take himself too seriously.

Richard says his father, a civilian administrator at a military base, was a natural leader who taught him how to be a Christian who lives out certain basic values. His parents were humble people who regularly welcomed "hobos" into their home, just three blocks from the railroad tracks. His father's model also taught him the deeper meaning of integrity, how to be content with himself. He notes happily that this solid sense of self comes in handy when he meets friends or parishioners from forty years ago, because he doesn't have to pretend to be someone else. He's just "Richard." And he especially resists being called "Monsignor," a title bestowed by the pope at the archbishop's recommendation but one that he resisted for years. He finally accepted the honor, he says, only because the people in his parish feel affirmed by the recognition of their beloved pastor.

The third of six children, Richard says that being part of his traditional Hispanic family also taught him to be part of a community rooted in tradition, guided by authority, and welcoming of diversity. But he is a post–Vatican II priest who believes, despite the deeply entrenched hierarchy of the Roman Catholic Church, that the real source of power within the church is in the laity. He understands that the days of "Father knows best" are passing, and whatever power he has as pastoral leader is a gift of the laypeople. Out of these roots, Richard's pastoral leadership demonstrates humility, hard work, clearly defined identity, and a very human connection to the members of the congregation. Richard's first principle of effective ministry and the foundation of his integrity is this: "Be a human being." Only then, he believes, can we learn to be Christians, and then ministers.

Richard's call to ordained ministry began to emerge in early adolescence, and he followed the Roman Catholic tradition of enrolling in minor seminary in high school. He was undecided about

how best to serve, though, until his college adviser told him that
the two most effective paths to changing the world were politics
and ministry. Being a pastor, the adviser went on to suggest, offered the most power to bring change, because "there you are dealing with ultimate realities." That advice set Richard on his path.

His early years in ministry were spent in rural churches, often quite poor, where he learned to deliver sermons, administer
the sacraments, manage church finances, and most of all, love the
people. After serving several parishes, he served a term as a missionary priest in Peru where, his brother Dennis recalls, "the water
was dirty, the fishing was sparse because of El Niño, and people
lived in cardboard boxes." And yet, even with those limitations,
he found a way to establish a medical clinic and feed breakfast to
two thousand children each day. During those missionary years,
he did not hesitate to speak up against the oppression of the state.
His archbishop was ultimately murdered, and it was rumored that
there was a contract out to kill a priest. Still, Richard stood his
ground and spoke out for his people.

When he returned from Peru, he was appointed vocations director for the archdiocese, building upon his comfort with young
people and his desire to strengthen the church. This experience
soon opened the door to his first term as chancellor and his deepening friendship with the previous archbishop, whose eventual
admission of sexual misconduct ultimately led to very different
paths for the two of them—Richard to a large parish, and the
archbishop to exile. It was from this large parish that the new
archbishop called him back to oversee the church's response to the
widespread scandal.

Speaking truth in love

Now as pastor of Risen Savior, Richard looks back on his career
in ministry—including the hardships of Peru, those difficult days
as chancellor, and his first months in this current parish—with
gratitude for the opportunities he has had to serve the church. "It's
the people," he says, "who are the church. Institutional problems
are real, and they can be heartbreaking, but the spirituality of the

people keeps me going. The people love God and are trying to live Christian lives, and that's what we must be helping them do."

Julie is one of those people in Risen Savior parish whose spirituality has been strengthened by Richard's ministry. She had been guarded in her engagement with the church for some years because of her disappointment in the priest who had performed her wedding, who was later accused of multiple cases of abuse. But she's been grateful for and encouraged by Richard's modest integrity and his clear commitment to the church's recovery from the sins of its past. When Richard set in place barriers to further failings, like abuse-prevention classes and windows in office doors, Julie's confidence in Richard's promises grew. "As skeptical as I am, I believed him when he said at mass that he could personally guarantee that no child would ever be abused at our church," she says, and Richard's ministry has helped her restore her enthusiasm for the church. She is now able to affirm God's dependable faithfulness in contrast to the betrayal of her former priest. "It was that person's human failing, and I wasn't going to let one priest shake our marriage or my faith. Besides, [Richard] is a very peaceful man who has never done anything that would steer us wrong. He sets the tone for the whole parish, and his tone is about love and acceptance and servitude."

Richard's pastoral leadership is not only one of tone, however. More important, he engages the community in addressing the pressing needs of those with whom he ministers. "To address and meet the needs of the people—that's the influence I've been called to have," he declares quietly. "It's not my job to meet my own needs or give them something prepackaged. I have to listen to what people are expressing and respond with the resources of the church." In this approach Richard embodies what Ronald Heifetz, founding director of the Center for Public Leadership at Harvard's Kennedy School of Government, calls "adaptive leadership." Heifetz argues that good leadership is much more than getting people to follow your vision. Such an approach is too leader-centered and risks becoming only a personality cult that can be used for either good or ill. At its best, he says, the first step of leadership must be "influencing the community to face its problems."[1] To be successful at such an endeavor, Heifetz continues, requires keen obser-

vational skills rooted in careful listening, combined with a courageous willingness to address hard issues in a way that lifts people's
actions to a higher plane.

Richard practices this kind of leadership, basing his work in
what Paul called in his letter to the Ephesians "speaking the truth
in love" (Eph. 4:15). In Peru, it allowed him to join with the people in figuring out how to feed children and provide medical care
in their poor community, while at the same time demonstrating to
them how to stand up to the injustice of a corrupt and frightening government. In both of his terms as chancellor, he acknowledged the shame of his own church, insisting that it confess its sin,
set aside its self-interest, and make essential changes for the good
of the people. In his current parish, he stepped quietly and confidently into his role as pastor to discouraged but still resourceful
people, listening to their hurts and leading them once again into
lively community with a renewed mission for the poor.

Richard's pastoral integrity is the foundation of his ability to
speak truth in love so compellingly. His integrity begins in his clear
sense of who he is as a man and a priest. "He's always consistent, always the same," Julie says of him, conveying a sentiment
expressed by several members of the parish. And the consistent
image is that of a gentle, loving, trustworthy, and very human
priest. As he goes about his pastoral duties, Richard displays what
Edwin Friedman called a "non-anxious presence," growing out
of his well-integrated identity, which Friedman would describe as
"self-differentiated."

Beyond that consistency, Richard's integrity is reinforced by
his fundamental honesty, which has fostered trust among parishioners of Risen Savior, just as it fostered trust among archbishops
and litigating attorneys over the years. His values, shaped first by
his family upbringing and later in formal priestly training, are re-
vealed in his leadership of meetings and masses, and convey core
teachings of the faith in his ordinary activities. "He's a force," says
Tes, a member of the parish council. "We know he is there, and we
know what he thinks and feels. He puts everything out there for
everyone to see, and he always reminds us, by his teaching and his
example, of who we are supposed to be as Christians."

"He's really cool about things," Ruth observes, recalling with appreciation how she and her husband, Ralph, have worked with him in their marriage-enrichment ministry for more than twenty-five years. "He knows when to keep his mouth shut and when to speak." Ralph quickly adds, "He's very low key, but also very astute. He's a strategic thinker—always three or four steps ahead of me. But he doesn't have to have his finger on everything, just gives guidance out of his own wise perspective. And what makes it so significant is that he's a very ordinary, down-to-earth people person."

Richard balances his gentle, loving side with his firm, truth-speaking side, in part by his deft collaboration with his staff. "Sometimes the best way to deliver a hard message is through one of the other staff people," Richard points out, a tactic that allows him to preserve his pastoral role with the people. "These decisions get made in our closed-door staff meetings where the clergy and lay staff and I have a very trusting relationship. They speak back to me very honestly, and there is a good give-and-take."

One area where this give-and-take with staff arose most intensely was in discussions about serving Hispanic and Spanish-speaking members. From his own upbringing, Richard understands the crucial importance of the Spanish language in affirming and preserving a rich cultural heritage. He was insistent, therefore, on scheduling a Spanish-language mass at the prime 8:00 a.m. time on Sundays to ensure a clear message of hospitality to those in the community who longed for that connection with their roots. His staff questioned the wisdom of this schedule, pointing out that most of those traditional Hispanic people were bilingual, and an English-language mass would reach a broader audience. "But I'm Hispanic," Richard says, "and I know how language and culture go hand in hand. So I'm not going to take a vote in the parish, because the Hispanics would lose." Rich, a parishioner and good friend, adds, "He knows how to pick his battles properly. Usually he's a great appeaser, not taking one side or the other. He should have been a politician, because somehow he appeases both sides. But when he thinks something's really important, as opposed to just setting the date for the church picnic, he will insist we do it right."

Humble authority

Richard's insistence on a Spanish mass at 8:00 a.m. on Sundays may not sound at first like the act of the gentle, self-effacing man people describe so often. Beneath the kindly persona, however, Richard carries a fierce commitment to values and responsibilities that grow out of his childhood training, his devout faith, and his understanding of his ordination vows. (And he does have a competitive streak, which comes out in situations like his weekly golf game with Rich, where the low scorer gets treated to a beer. Richard's competitiveness even led to a broken ankle in a parish softball game one time!) Most of the time, though, his is a humble authority, not demanding or directive. But this story of the Spanish-language mass reveals the integrity with which Richard weaves together the essential humanness he prizes with the necessary authority he believes is required by his office to uphold certain fundamental principles.

As a member of Richard's staff, Kenn appreciates the way Richard expresses his own thoughts while affirming the ideas and gifts of others. He says Richard never overlooks anyone's gifts, and he doesn't micromanage those with whom he works. He gives people tasks and allows them to find their own ways of accomplishing them. He expects from people exactly what he expects from himself: "being true to oneself and serving people as best we can." Kenn says that Richard's philosophy of ministry has become the heart of the parish, but as influential as he is, Richard does not propagate "yes men." He is the furthest thing from a dictator, Kenn insists, allowing staff to judge situations for themselves, try new things, and keep the ministries of the church fresh. "He accepts us for who we are, loves us for who we are. He can be disappointed or hurt by people around him, but he puts it in context."

As Kenn talked of Richard's leadership, I was reminded of Jim Collins's description of "Level 5" leaders, people at the helm of the outstanding businesses profiled in his best-selling book *Good to Great.* Collins found in the leaders of these extraordinary businesses a certain humility that gives credit to others for things that succeed and takes personal responsibility for failures that inevitably occur. Richard understands very well the importance of humility, contrasting it with pride, which he says is "the root of the slippery slope of vice, while humility is the beginning of the slippery slope of virtue." Kenn respectfully summarizes Richard's exercise of humble authority: "Richard is a remarkable leader because he doesn't come across as a leader. It's all for the benefit of the parish and the glory of God."

Looking forward to celebrating the fortieth anniversary of his ordination to the priesthood next year, Richard expects to serve as a pastor for six more years. He is still mentally sharp and physically fit, but he says his ministry has changed in recent years. He says he "used to prepare homilies, but now I share my faith. I used to say prayers; now I pray." He summarizes his ministry these days as "all spiritual guidance." His colleagues in ministry, mostly laypeople and volunteers, carry out the programs of the church. He's a pastor in the truest sense, guiding people through the difficult questions of faith and sustaining them through the complexities of life's joys and troubles. The day before our first interview, he had planned to go to lunch by himself at noon, but as he was walking out the door, he was flagged down by a man who needed Richard's prayer because he was on the verge of losing his family. "If I can't miss a lunch occasionally to comfort a man in such distress, I wouldn't be much of a priest," he says.

He is a disciplined man, despite such occasional detours. He credits his father for teaching him how to work—think it out, prepare, do it in a timely fashion, bring it to an end. He takes Wednesdays off religiously (if I may use that word), often playing a round of golf or flying his plane around the countryside, and he takes his allotted vacation every year. He eats three regular, well-balanced meals daily, uses alcohol in moderation, and never has second helpings or snacks between meals. He's in bed by ten each night, gets eight hours of sleep, exercises regularly, and has a physical exam every six months. He nurtures a playful sense of humor and reads the comics in the newspaper every morning.

He cherishes quiet times listening to music, and he begins each day with prayer based in Scripture and liturgy, and he reviews his schedule in his PDA. He embraces what Jesuit priest Jean-Pierre de Caussade described as "the sacrament of the present mo-ment,"[2] staying focused on the present and rarely thinking about yesterday or fretting about tomorrow. He enjoys his family, his personal relationships, and friendship with a few other priests, in-cluding the archbishop, with whom he has vacationed in Italy. He misses his parents, who have died in recent years, and he lives in the family home, where he had moved to nurse his father through his final illness. Richard can navigate any social situation with grace, but he knows who he is: a simple parish priest who usually wears his brother's hand-me-down clothes when he's not wearing his clerical collar.

These patterns sustain his faith and his fitness, helping preserve his humanity while undergirding the authority of his ministry and the integrity on which that authority is based. Certainly, the personal disciplines have sustained his body and his spirit for the varied demanding ministries he has performed. He reflects with wonder on the fact that he was ordained with five other men, "and now I'm the only one left still serving in ministry. They were smart-er, holier. How is it that God has preserved me?" But Richard's diligent practice of faith, his dedication to core values, and his de-termination to be true to himself are the primary ingredients of the fertile soil that brings fruitfulness to his work as pastoral leader as well. Growth, healing, comfort, vocation, mercy for the poor, the pursuit of justice—all these have emerged from Richard's faith-ful ministry and continue to flourish through the ministrations of those he serves.

Richard's question is one we all might ask ourselves. How is it that a modest man from an ordinary family becomes a person of such well-differentiated integrity and enduring impact? After all, the values that he lives are the values that all Christians espouse. His self-discipline may be stronger than most, but anyone could follow such a schedule and sustain clerical fitness if they were so inclined. Psychologists might examine ego strength and resilience fostered by the dynamics of his family of origin. Biogenetic make-up surely plays a role. But lots of people have good genes and good parents, good Christian values and good luck.

God's generous providence must also be part of the equation. This is not to suggest some simplistic predestination that imagines a divine plan for a fellow named Richard. But the nature-versus-nurture question is not sufficient. Providence makes room for a loving spirit that Richard acknowledges "is always there, inspirational, and merciful. When I realize that I'm not the center and God *is* in the center," he says, "it makes a difference." For whatever reason, Richard is able to see, and to receive, God's providence in his life. And his willingness to receive into his humanity the gifts of vocation, discipline, integrity, and especially the gift of effective pastoral leadership that grows from those more basic gifts, makes him particularly equipped to foster receptivity to God's grace in individual people and the church as a whole.

HELPING PEOPLE DISCOVER THEIR MINISTRY

Six months after she left her ministry with Immanuel Church, Joyce realized how terribly exhausted she had been. "I'm not sure I did a very good job there," she says. "I was tap-dancing all the time, trying to keep ministry alive and bring people along. But their sense of ownership wasn't really there." She's now serving in a national post for her denomination, but she's clear that if she returns to the parish, she'll do things differently. "I would not say, 'Let's do this. Come on, I'll show you how.' Instead, I would focus on helping folks discover their own sense of ministry and how we might work that out. It would be their impetus, not mine."

The harvest

Richard's leadership has had an enormous impact on the body of Christ wherever he has served. In his present parish, as well as in previous ministries, the growth in numbers and expansion of facilities are the most tangible results of his work. Far more important, though, is the fact that out of his own well-differentiated integrity he has taught the church, both parish and diocese, to face its own dark shadows with courage to cultivate the elements of fruitfulness that had been lying fallow. In his ministries, he has fostered the healing of profound brokenness and the transformation of the church from a defensive body filled with shame to a church more confident in its ability to fulfill its mission to serve a world of pressing needs.

Richard is, of course, a servant leader. Jesus talked often about the first being last and the necessity of serving, and his radical act of washing his disciples' feet on the night before his arrest showed the way of servant leadership. Robert Greenleaf and others have interpreted servant leadership more comprehensively, offering it as a model for conveying authority with a humility that empowers others. In Greenleaf's words, such leadership "begins with the natural feeling that one wants to serve, to serve first" (as opposed to wanting to be a leader first). From that point, then, the effectiveness of servant leadership is measured by this test: "Do those served grow as persons; do they, *while being served*, become healthier, wiser, freer, more autonomous, more likely themselves to become servants? *And*, what is the effect on the least privileged in society; will they benefit, or, at least, not be further deprived?"[3]

Many in his parish would acknowledge that when Richard invites people into a deeper life in Christ, one that displays greater generosity and goodness, the response is usually positive and concrete. That's one reason why Risen Savior has been able in the past nine years to undertake a major building renovation and erect a new parish hall for an expanded youth and family program while parishioners have increased their charitable outreach to several programs for the poor. And when the archbishop asked for his help financing a new church for a historic but very poor immigrant parish whose building was collapsing, Richard quickly persuaded his church to pledge fifty thousand dollars while also enlisting other parishes in the cause. Richard doesn't command or cajole such responses. He aspires to high standards, and he leads by example, influencing others to follow. Service fosters service.

On a more personal level, everyone I talked with about Richard's pastoral leadership identified three rich fruits that will endure within the people touched by his ministry. All agreed that Richard has fostered in people a deeper love of the church, a greater awareness and willingness to exercise their own gifts, and a stronger determination to serve the poor.

Tes explains the reason she became so involved in several ministries of the parish: "He reminds us that through our baptism we are called to serve, to help those who can't help themselves, like feeding the hungry or teaching children. And then, being active in the church reminds us why we are here. It's eye-opening to see the needs that are out there." Tes, like the entire parish that Richard serves, is inspired by the example of his service to exercise her own service to others. "Sometimes we don't like to hear the truth. We get tired. Daily obligations can get in the way. But his gentle reminders inspire us to do more."

"People are looking for spirituality," Richard says, "trying to find ways of living out their religion in daily life. I try through my preaching to help people see how they are gifted—that's probably the most common theme in my homilies." He also understands that the best way to understand people's gifts is to be in relationship with them. "People will tell you about their own gifts if you listen to them. Then it's a matter of inviting them to use those gifts in some way."

In this endeavor, Tes believes that Richard is carrying on what his predecessor started, identifying and bringing out the strengths of the people and getting them involved in serving the church and the world. "He calls himself a sacramental shepherd—focusing on administering the sacraments and letting the people run the church." Richard's view of the church is, in fact, very much one of empowering and equipping people to be ministers themselves. "All you have to do," he says, "is cultivate the gifts that are here. You don't have to plant new seeds. It pains me when new pastors come in and change everything within weeks. I came and built upon the foundation that was here."

This attentiveness to others plays out in the warm hospitality of the church, and Julie thinks that the welcoming spirit in the parish will never change. "Risen Savior is a place where people are respected for who they are, not how much they have or what their mental capabilities may be. Everyone has a valid place there. Richard always thanks people, is always appreciative. He doesn't take anything for granted." She speaks compellingly of this openness and appreciation, reflecting on the welcome her own special-needs child has received as an altar server. "They even removed the cry room from the church when we remodeled. Everyone is welcome in the church, not just the well-behaved."

"The spirit of the people will definitely last," Ruth adds. "They are going to continue to demand that things keep going, and they'll do the work. Monsignor has taught us to be in ministry and always move ahead. Ministry just becomes a part of who you are because it's in giving that you receive." She says she learned that lesson most clearly from Richard, and it's easy to see why. The gifts Richard has received—vocation and family and rich pastoral experience, which he has formed with persistent discipline into an inspiring strength for service built upon fundamental Christian values—sustain his spirit and his ministry. Now those gifts will germinate in the lives of generations to come. "I think even if Attila the Hun comes after me as pastor," Richard says with a smile, "the people will still be here and the sense of welcome and belonging will remain. They will have confidence in their own individual gifts as well as the gift of community in the church. And out of that wonderful community the commitment to outreach will endure."

chapter 3

Practicing Possibilities

• *Russell* •

L anky and laconic, Russell is still extremely fit in his seventy-ninth year of life. He joined me at the Village Inn directly from his daily workout at the gym; he still runs several times a week. As our coffee and his apple pie á la mode arrived at the table, he offered a simple blessing for our food and conversation. He's fit not only physically, but mentally and spiritually as well. And he's still a pastor, even though he retired from full-time ministry more than ten years ago. (He avoids the word "retirement," calling his life these days "redirected living"—always thinking new thoughts.)

After a few minutes of catching up on our lives, he begins to tell me about his long and fruitful ministry at Faith Church. Thinking back to the beginning nearly forty-five years ago, he recalls being quite determined to serve a small church when he was invited in 1964 to interview with Faith about becoming the congregation's new pastor. "If you want someone to build a large church, don't call me," he declared in his first meeting with the three-hundred-member parish. That suited the members just fine, and so Russell and his wife, Elaine, packed their meager belongings back in South Dakota, where he had been an associate pastor since leaving seminary, and they headed west.

When he retired thirty-three years later, Russell was still a small-church pastor. Never mind that the congregation had more than one thousand people in worship most Sundays and was one of the largest parishes in the synod. It was people that Russell cared about, and he cared for each member in his flock as attentively as any small-church pastor. Everyone still got a birthday phone call, and newcomers got a home visit before joining. People were encouraged to join small groups with which they met regularly, and these group members knew one another's names and lives and questions. There was a small-church feel of comfortable familiarity to worship on Sundays—in all three services! But looking back on the growth and changes that came during his pastoral leadership, Russell smiles about the way the church developed over the years and quietly admits, "Of course, I changed my thinking."

Russell's ministry is marked by such changes in thinking, and the changes he brought to the congregation and the people he served continue to unfold, sometimes in surprising and unintended ways. The changes in thinking began to emerge when his first big challenge arose in 1968. He started out like any good small-church pastor, calling on loyal members to get acquainted as well as visiting neighbors to invite them to church. Despite his bumper sticker opposing the war in Vietnam, most of the congregation warmed to him and Elaine and their two daughters—except the ones who began speaking in tongues. By 1968 the glossolalia faction had begun to question his authority, while at the same time a growing minority of the congregation was ready to brand him a "bad leader," because he was challenging the unwritten rule of many churches: "But we've always done it this way." He remembers the attacks and the uncertainty of those times with pain, and he remains grateful for the bishop's intervention when, after a series of listening conferences with disenchanted members, he came to Russell's defense and insisted he remain the pastor. That encounter deepened his longstanding appreciation for the denomination, despite his frustration with some national trends in the church and his growing distance from fellow pastors who suspected he was just building his own kingdom.

Eldon, the president of the congregation when Russell was called to Faith, recalls that this pastor did not really seem to be a strong leader at first. Faith Church was his first solo pastorate, and he got in a little trouble early on by preaching against the Vietnam War. "He got off on the wrong foot; or maybe, in hindsight, it was the right foot," Eldon says. Even at that early stage of his ministry, Russell was demonstrating his independence of mind and commitment to his understanding of God's call, qualities that would appear again and again throughout his ministry and would come to pervade the congregation's life as well.

Those early crises during his first six years of this ministry—controversy about his stance toward the war and factionalism around speaking in tongues—brought Russell up short. He thought seriously about resigning from Faith to go find a church that might be a better fit. But with the bishop's support and the encouragement of some of his lay leaders, he instead went off to Robert Schuller's brand-new Institute of Leadership in Garden Grove, California. Schuller's television ministry at the Crystal Cathedral was regarded with some suspicion among mainline churches in those days. But Russell had long been open to creative approaches, and Schuller's presentation of "possibility thinking" was intriguing to him, even if it meant his denominational colleagues began labeling him a "Schullerite."

The groundwork for Russell's attraction to "possibility thinking" had been laid during his college years when he attended a lecture by Sam Shoemaker, the spiritual mentor of Bill Wilson, who founded Alcoholics Anonymous. Shoemaker was an evangelical, and he lit a fire in Russell that took him away from his more traditional roots to a focus on evangelism for his ministry. While in seminary, Russell requested permission to do an internship with Shoemaker in Pittsburgh, but his denomination required that he be placed in one of its own churches, and Shoemaker was an Episcopalian. Russell persisted and finally arranged to be assigned to one of his own denomination's churches in the neighborhood but to do his actual work in Shoemaker's parish. So began a lifelong pattern of testing the limits of church structures.

Russell's journey to Garden Grove was the catalyst that re-shaped his ministry for the next thirty years. First and most impor-tant, he came to understand in the institute's sessions the power of focusing on possibilities. He realized that effective ministry could begin by building upon the untapped potential of people. The sec-ond emphasis, growing out of the first and seasoned by surviving those years of controversy, came from a decision to "think long term" about his ministry.

These two major changes prompted Russell to see his own role as a leader differently. He remembers Lyle Schaller, another of his mentors, once asking him, "Russell, are you the leader in this church?" When he replied rather contritely, "I don't know," Schaller insisted, "Russell, you'd better know." As he reflects on that exchange now, Russell realizes that before that encounter, he had always thought of himself as more of a servant. "It took me a long time to get comfortable with the notion of being a servant-leader." Over the course of many years, Russell had to learn how to build a staff and train lay leaders, eventually becoming "more comfortable in large-church pastor clothes." So his pastoral excel-lence was born in his early troubles, fostered by the encourage-ment of nontraditional mentors, and brought to flower by a grow-ing awareness of his very real gifts in ministry. Channeling those gifts into a long-term strategy that built upon the possibilities of people became his fundamental approach to ministry.

A hopeful vision

Building upon possibilities begins with learning to think positively and incorporating those positive thought patterns into a disci-plined way of life. Russell had long admired the teachings of Nor-man Vincent Peale and still cherishes a photo of him and Elaine together with Dr. and Mrs. Peale, taken on a visit to the Marble Collegiate Church in Manhattan. But in his time with Robert Schuller in 1972 and in several follow-up sessions over the years, Russell began to understand more fully that people need some-thing to cling to that gives their life meaning and joy and direction.

Russell credits Schuller with "reshaping and putting substance into what I didn't have before." Vern, who with his wife, Vicki, became a member of Faith because of Russell's leadership, summarized their attraction to Russell's style: "People are beaten down enough in their day-to-day living. They need to be lifted up."

Russell's ministry came to embody hopefulness, and that spirit became increasingly evident in his leadership, his teaching, and his personal life. Eldon remembers clearly how, as finance chairman, he did a financial study when Faith's members were first considering the possibility of moving from their old location to a new site on the edge of town. "I proved without a doubt we *could not* do it." But Russell was confident in his vision, which he believed to be God's vision for the future of the church. So with the support of a small group of dedicated believers, Russell and Eldon and the other leaders moved ahead anyway, building the first phase of the new church in the middle of a vast field of sagebrush. And the people came, the congregation growing by more than a third in the first couple of years.

Russell's positive vision for the church as an institution grew out of a practical hope for people's lives, and this hope pervaded the air of the parish. Vern found Russell's attitude refreshingly different from his own experience of church leadership, which he had experienced most fully in preaching that "took people to the dock and threw them in so they could be rescued." Russell was not like the pastor of Vern's own confirmation class, "bursting with law and hiding gospel in his back pocket," Vern says. That man's approach had been "conform or exit,"—so Vern exited. In contrast, there was an absence of judging and an emphasis on the positive in Russell's leadership, and out of such differences came an enthusiastic spirit that drew people like Vern and Vicki in from a variety of religious traditions, as well as from the ranks of those unaffiliated with any religious group. "We probably wouldn't have been church members if it weren't for Russell," Vicki adds.

Eldon believes it was Russell's positive confidence in people that permitted him to empower others to amazing accomplishments. He came to understand, with Russell as his pastor, that "if you really believe in something, you can do it," whether building a new church despite the financial projections, or surviving the loss of a beloved wife (an experience which Eldon and Russell shared). Having now left Faith Church, Eldon says he is "looking for a church like Faith used to be." He's still on a hopeful journey, eager to embrace the possibilities of this life as he longs to learn more about the road ahead.

Although he has never used the term, Russell's approach to ministry is built upon the principles of positive psychology. Most fully described by Martin Seligman at the University of Pennsylvania, positive psychology is "founded on the belief that people want to lead meaningful and fulfilling lives, to cultivate what is best within themselves, and to enhance their experiences of love, work, and play."[1] Positive psychology is the still-emerging theoretical underpinning of both Peale's "power of positive thinking" and Schuller's "possibility thinking."

In the religious realm, of course, positive psychology has much in common with the theology of hope, which emerged in the 1960s in the writings of Jurgen Moltmann and others. This school of theology gives considerable attention to happiness in this life but retains the central significance of sin and judgment in its eschatological framework that positive psychology tends to downplay. Moltmann and his colleagues, along with the psychologists, did emphasize the need for Christians to work at improving the individual's situation while also fostering worldly happiness and building better institutions, including churches.

Unbridled reliance upon positive psychology in the religious realm has unfortunately fostered in some quarters today's "prosperity gospel" preachers. These misguided leaders have suggested not only that God wants good things for Christians, but also that if you believe strongly enough and trust fully enough, God will reward you with material possessions, good health, and so on. The prosperity gospel, which too often neglects the eschatological awareness of the theology of hope, has led some believers to disastrous consequences and has propelled some preachers into questionable practices. Russell's embrace of positive psychology never crossed the line into such errors, and the members of Faith Church still seem clear about the limits of possibility thinking.

Despite the strong psychological theme in Russell's emerging version of the gospel, he remained a deeply faithful man whose biblical foundation was often more implicit than explicit. But he trusted God while embracing this life to the fullest. He recalls with a smile a story Schuller once told about how he applied his faith to the practical necessities of life. Schuller had been planning to go on vacation, and suddenly a crisis arose in the church that threatened to interfere with his plans. Schuller told of sitting in his chair in his study and praying about what to do when there came into his mind the words of Jesus: "I will build my church." Immediately Schuller knew what to do. "OK, Lord," he said, "you stay here and build your church, and I'll go on vacation." While the story brought laughter to the seminar room full of pastors, the point of the story was clear to Russell. He must do his part *and* trust God to be the author of all success. In that trust was the source of his hope.

Thinking long term

The decision to build his ministry upon the principles of positive thinking led quite naturally to adopting a long-term strategy for his vocation. The ups and downs of ministry are as common as the changing seasons and the rise and fall of the stock market. Beginning to comprehend this reality as a still relatively young man, Russell realized that he should stay at Faith Church for the long haul.

A ministry of thirty-three years is remarkable in today's world of widespread mobility and even disposability. In Russell's case, as for many parish pastors, there were also times of terrible stress—the attacks and factions in his early years, the periods of financial anxiety as the church reached beyond its means, the death of his first wife, Elaine. Surviving such hardship is not easy, particularly in the very public role of pastor. But when he was asked by a colleague what he would do after the death of his wife, he said, "I plan to keep on doing my pastoral ministry." His friend replied, "Of course. That is what you are for." Russell always knew who he was, and so did others. He was, and still is, a pastor. Beyond that, however, what were the keys to his ability to endure and stay fresh in a long-term parish ministry?

First, he stayed physically fit. Unlike most clergy—as we learn from recent disturbing reports about the high rates of obesity, lack of exercise, poor diet, diabetes, and high blood pressure among clergy—Russell took care of his body. He worked out at the gym regularly, ran often in the mountains near his home, and ate healthful meals (with occasional dispensation for pie á la mode).

Second, throughout his ministry, but especially in the days of tension and even attack, he recognized the need for supportive peers. Russell has regularly been buoyed by covenant groups of colleagues who challenged and respected and encouraged him, and for a time I was one of his regular lunch companions, along with the local rabbi and a United Methodist pastor in town. His trips to Robert Schuller's Leadership Institutes were also part of this strategy of constructing intentional support systems. Mentors at the institute and pastors from around the country shared ideas and enthusiasm for ministry with him, and he looked forward to being out of town in a different setting to recharge his batteries. He sometimes took along a lay leader from his congregation to help expand the impact of new ideas and to foster sustaining structures when he returned home.

More than anything else, though, Russell endured by staying out of ruts. He stayed fresh by developing new approaches to worship, starting new Bible studies, finding new people to be members and friends, reading new books, and trying out new ideas. Being a long-distance runner was a metaphor for his growth in faith and his practice of ministry—it was a marathon and not a sprint. A central strategy for his practice of hope, then, was a deep commitment to constant learning. When I told him over coffee that I had always been impressed with his unrelenting curiosity, his wife, Helen, let out a loud sigh and said, "Oh yes, he asks *so* many questions! His middle initial is C, and I'm sure that doesn't stand for Curtis, like he says, but Curious." Russell admits to an insatiable inquisitiveness, and he credits Lyle Schaller with telling him that the most important question in the world is, "How come?"

What's more, Russell often invited questions and different points of view from others as well. He encouraged people to think beyond the boundaries of tradition in faith and church life. He was even tolerant of dissent, although there came times, such as with the "speakers in tongues," when he drew boundaries. But he experimented and explored, and he invited others to do so as well. He read widely and urged church leaders and members alike to be well informed about their faith and its history.

Through many changes and throughout the congregation's growth, however, Russell clung tenaciously to a strong central vision and stayed "on message." John and Kris are clear that God was active in Russell's leadership, notably through the clarity of Russell's vision, which fostered his ministry's initiatives. They cite his strong grounding in Scripture and his eagerness to involve people in Bible studies over the years. His leadership was, they believe, always inviting and suggestive: "If you are searching, why don't you try this study?" The church was not "Russell-centered," they insist, but Christ-centered.

Eldon told me that he had recently visited a church where Russell was guest preaching and saw that he was still "showing people a loving God. This determination he has, what he believes he must pass on—he can't help himself." Of course, that sometimes meant that the church lost members too. In the early years of Russell's ministry, Eldon recalls, some who had been active for years left, complaining, "I came to hear the gospel, but all I got was a counseling session." But as Vern notes, Russell's determination was to address the practical issues of a Christian's daily life in a hopeful and positive spirit, and that was central to his mission of nurturing and leading a growing people of faith.

Russell's mentors in faith and practice—Robert Schuller, Lyle Schaller, Norman Vincent Peale, Philip Yancey, Henri Nouwen—all invited open thinking while remaining firmly rooted in biblical roots and faithful practice. In his own constant professional development, Russell notes, the key question was always, "What would help me be a better pastor?" Yes, he was, as many who know him would attest, a bit of a workaholic. But his persistence created an enduring impact. "He was a serial planner," Vern observes, "and he must have had dogged determination to survive. But God was in all the caring and nurturing." John and Kris point out that despite some changes in the congregation in the past ten years, the core vision and mission statements have not changed. The big push this year is evangelism, expanding the church of Christ, and that's not much different from the emphasis during Russell's years.

Russell always knew his trust must be in God, but he learned early in ministry that God does not usually bring harvests overnight. Russell had originally assumed that his career would be marked by a series of shorter pastorates. In his early years of ministry, Schuller had encouraged him to think more carefully about the next forty years of his ministry as well as the long-term life and ministry of the congregation. As he did so, Russell realized that he must learn to overcome discouragement, practice endurance, and persevere through the hard times. Certainly his effectiveness in implementing the practical skills of a hopeful ministry also contributed to his endurance, eventually leading him to conclude that he was "in the right place at the right time—it was a new sense of calling." He realized that Faith Church could be his locus for ministry for many years. But as the years unfolded, he also came to understand more deeply that he could be effective in ministry over the long term only if he maintained healthy relationships with people.

Emotionally intelligent leadership

At the core of his ministry, and a key to his strategy of achieving possibilities over a thirty-three-year period, was his consistently giving priority to personal relationships with people. He remained a small-church pastor at heart, and he "stayed in touch" with his people, as Rabbi Edwin Friedman called leaders to do. Russell is not an especially sociable man. His reserved manner is consistent with his Scandinavian heritage and his midwestern manners. But interest in others shines in his eyes, and his ready willingness to respond to their needs brings him close to those he meets. John and Kris recall with great fondness the guidance and support he gave them as Kris made the transition from her Catholic upbringing to becoming a Protestant with her husband. She remembers him as a "very quiet presence" who got them involved in a Bethel Bible Study and then sensitively coached her in explaining this new life in faith to her skeptical mother, who had stopped talking to her for six months. Eldon grows quiet as he remembers with sad appreciation Russell's pastoral care during the time of his first wife's dying. Vern adds, "He was a people person whose ministry was from the heart."

The model for Russell's commitment to person-centered ministry is readily found in Scripture. Reading Paul's powerful letters to the early church, one is struck not only by the deep theological wisdom and straightforward ethical declarations contained in those missives, but also by the very human caring Paul expresses. Paul was a church planter who practiced short-term ministries, but he seems still to have maintained long-term relationships. To his friend Philemon, Paul writes, for example, "I have indeed received much joy and encouragement from your love, because the hearts of the saints have been refreshed through you, my brother." Such openly expressed love led, I suspect, to Philemon's welcoming the errant slave Onesimus home. To the church in Rome, Paul lifts up Prisca and Aquila, "who risked their necks for my life," and countless others whom he has admired and loved, and who are deserving of "a holy kiss." Most of Paul's letters contain personal greetings and fond reminiscences like these, and it is out of such tender pastoral caring that Paul ministered. Paul knew his people, deepening that knowledge with common toil, shared sacrifice, and heartfelt affection.

Russell combined in his ministry the pastoral sensitivity of the apostle Paul with a modern psychological understanding about the importance of positive personal relationships in building and leading a vital community. His empathy toward people in the parish and his own self-awareness, motivation, and ability to manage his relationships with others are all signs of an "emotional intelligence," which Daniel Goleman has described in his book of that name. Applying his theory to the practice of leadership in his book *Primal Leadership,* coauthored with Richard Boyatzis and Annie McKee, Goleman goes further to describe a style of leadership that creates resonance with those being led. Resonance in an organization, these authors believe, is a principal sign that the leader and the people are on the same page, feeling themselves to be in harmony as they live and work together addressing their common mission.

The competencies of emotionally intelligent leaders, according to Goleman and his colleagues, include self-awareness (emotional self-awareness, accurate self-assessment, self-confidence); self-management (emotional self-control, transparency, adaptability, achievement, initiative, optimism); social awareness (empathy, organizational awareness, service); and relationship management (inspirational leadership, influence, developing others, change catalyst, conflict management, building bonds, teamwork and collaboration).[2]

Russell has come to know himself fairly well over the years, aided by openness to feedback from friends and colleagues and his voracious reading habits. In particular, his "self-management" grows out of his early recognition of his own sense of personal inadequacy. He chose to address his lack of self-confidence, he says, by becoming a "continual learner, always striving to be a better husband, a more faithful follower of Christ, a better preacher." He believes his life has always been about constant renewal, and he cites Dallas Willard's book *Renovation of the Heart* as an example of the practical, step-by-step improvements he has practiced in his own life to overcome this sense of inadequacy. His attraction to "possibility thinking" became the primary framework for building a new sense of optimism upon which he could build his work.

Russell also came to know how to "stay in touch" and to understand the effects of those connections in his particular setting, a sign of both his "social awareness" and his "relationship management." John and Kris remain deeply grateful to him for his gentle guidance during her religious transition, and as a number of recent studies about the psychology of gratitude have shown, grateful people feel strongly connected to the giver and become more generous themselves. For Vern and Vicki, Russell was a graceful teacher of the faith who encouraged them to continue to read and grow in their spiritual lives. For others, like Eldon, connections were formed through the routine acts of ministry in times of crisis, such as Russell's comforting care during the death of Eldon's wife, or even the companionship born of shared work in building a church.

Observation of his ministry and the tangible results of his leadership show that Russell was an adept practitioner of the competencies necessary for emotionally intelligent leadership. The growth of the congregation and the harmonious spirit of Faith Church during Russell's term as pastor could have been a case study for the resonance that Goleman and his colleagues affirm. This rich relational context became the loam out of which have emerged the fruitful lives of countless individuals and the continuing vital life of Faith Church.

I'LL GIVE IT ALL I'VE GOT

"I felt called to full-time Christian service in high school," Joan recalls, "so I studied Christian education in college, which was the only real possibility for women in those days. And then I married a preacher, which I guess was the other option for ministry available to women of my generation." But Joan's sense of call continued to nag at her, and after several secular jobs, she eventually pursued her denomination's alternate track to ministry. "I realized that I would be fifty-five when I completed the process, but then I thought, 'Well, I'll be fifty-five anyway, so why not?'"

So she persisted, and after being ordained an elder, she served in a couple of parish ministries and as a district superintendent until she took early retirement to care for her husband in his final years of ill health. Now in her mid-seventies, she observes, "This is not the world I grew up in," so she keeps learning and looking for new ways to serve. She has been associate pastor of a small-town congregation for five years and continues to adapt her work to the needs of the parish. "Along with being temporary business manager since our administrator resigned, right now my number-one goal is to help our new minister succeed as pastor of this church. That's my current call, and I'll give it all I've got."

A consequential ministry

Still, although he is appreciated by many and loved by some, Russell is not idolized by his former parishioners. And there were certainly those who left Faith Church during the course of his ministry, like the woman who withdrew her membership saying she came to be fed by Scripture and all she got was a counseling session. People see his faults, and no one at Faith or in its diaspora—the "Faith alumni group," as one former member called it—seems ready to canonize him. Yet the powerful impact of his ministry persists among those he served.

He doesn't take undue pride in the impact of his work. In fact, he's quite humble about his contributions. "Honestly, between you and me, I feel that I don't know very much," he confesses, displaying once again both his humility and his underlying struggle with self-confidence. Yet the significance of this large congregation in the community and the influence of Russell's ministry there are most readily seen in two major ways. First, he set the church on a path of growth that continues, after a brief period of transition early in the term of his successor, to this day. The church's distinction is not just in the beauty of the buildings or the number of people on the rolls, though those buildings and numbers should not be dismissed. But the church remains a vital spiritual home for more than two thousand people who experience in its life and ministry the meaning and work of the body of Christ. Even more important for people like Eldon and Vern, the fact that they came to know and practice their faith more deeply has made a significant difference in the way they live their lives. Eldon speaks for many of them when he says, "Being with [Russell] all those years had a major effect on me, and much of what I am now is because of those years with him."

What's more, many of the members of Faith, present and past, continue their own lively journeys of faith, practicing the principles and embracing the beliefs and values they first learned from Russell. Open and inquisitive thinking, a hopeful spirit, practicing faith in practical religious disciplines—these remain identifying marks of those who enjoyed Russell's pastoral leadership, whether they remain members of Faith Church or have gone on to other church homes in their journeys of faith. "He allowed us to change and grow in spiritual understanding," Vern says, surrounded by materials he is using in preparing a lesson from Phyllis Tickle's new book, which he will teach next Sunday in a United Methodist congregation that he and Vicki now attend. The growth and change, and especially the earnest seeking, continue.

Faith Church, meanwhile, remains a strong and lively congregation, though it has made some curious changes of its own since Russell retired. There have been, in fact, some unintended consequences growing from the directions of his leadership. The church has moved from one denominational branch of its tradition to another under the vigorous leadership of his successor, Bruce. Most would agree that the congregation has become more conservative; some say it has become more authoritarian. But in many ways the parish, despite the departure of a number of its longtime members as a result of that shift in denominational identity, has resumed its pattern of growth and continues to explore new programs and possibilities that began under Russell's leadership. It remains, in the words of John, a three-time former president of the congregation who is a twenty-six-year member of the parish, "an outlier" with a strong commitment to evangelism and to being "Christ's church, not Russell's or Bruce's or any other leader's."

Bruce, who has now been pastor of Faith Church for more than ten years, is clear that the congregation has always gone its own way and hadn't been very invested in its former denominational identity for many years. Long before Bruce came to Faith, the parish didn't use denominational curriculum materials, and Russell and the other pastors seldom attended clergy gatherings. He sees Russell as almost nondenominational in leadership, although acknowledging that Russell leaned to the left side of the aisle while he leans to the right. "But Faith never depended on the denomination for our marching orders, and that was true in Russell's day as well," he says. As Bruce sees it, Faith Church remains an independent-minded congregation that still affirms exactly the same mission statement that guided its life during Russell's long ministry.

When he came to the church, he found a group of folk who clung to Russell's vision and others who wanted to try new directions. And so the church remains lively in its searching and dedicated to following Christ in its own way, even as it continues to support many of the community ministries begun under Russell's leadership and maintains its commitment to small groups while reaching out in a variety of new ways.

Pastoral relationships as strong as Russell's do not go away overnight, and they sometimes foster attachments that are difficult to alter or break. It is hard to know to what extent those who left Faith Church when the congregation shifted its denominational connection did so because of their own theological and social beliefs, or out of pure denominational loyalty. One could even wonder whether some people left because of a continuing transferential attachment to Russell that interfered with their ability to connect with the new pastor. I see no evidence, though, that Russell fostered such unhealthy attachments or encouraged resistance to Bruce's leadership. Relationships carry their own power, and the people of Faith were accustomed to a satisfying and familiar pastoral relationship with Russell that could no longer continue after he left. So having learned the importance of seeking and self-direction, some of them moved on.

What did not happen, though, is also significant. It is interesting to observe the failed transition in pastoral leadership in the church of Russell's mentor, Robert Schuller. When Schuller's son, the designated successor to his father, attempted to lead the church in a more orthodox, explicitly biblically based direction, not unlike the direction Faith Church took under Bruce's leadership, conflict arose that ultimately resulted in the senior Schuller's removing his son from leadership. Schuller's daughter then became the pastor and the Crystal Cathedral subsequently filed for bankruptcy protection. Russell, on the other hand, stayed out of the tensions that arose in the transition at Faith Church, and as a result, he and Bruce, as well as the members who stayed and the members who left, have all managed to continue their lively journeys of faith and service.

Russell's leadership was characterized by innovation and change—practicing possibilities. He modeled it in his wide reading, his constant questions, and his exploration of nontraditional (at least for a mainline Protestant pastor) training and professional growth experiences. As John said, Russell was an "outlier," and as a result, so was Faith Church. Some of Russell's denominational colleagues were not very tolerant of his role models and his distancing from their gatherings, but Russell seemed not to mind, saying, "I had to rise above the need for peer approval." He was clear about his own faith and his own vision for the church's future. When his bishop learned recently that Russell was now doing part-time ministry at a church of a different denomination in town, he said, "Yes, that's Russell—doing his own thing."

John, who with his wife, Kris, remains a leader in Faith Church, continues to demonstrate the thoughtful searching that Russell modeled. He was recently confronted with a cancer diagnosis that at first appeared life-threatening. After successful treatment led to a remission, he wrote of the testing of faith that this mortal encounter provoked. John is a scientist, and his reflections straddle the scientific world of his work and the world of faith where Russell led him. As John put it in his essay, he has learned not only to challenge deeply his own faith, but also to "doubt my doubts" as he embraces God's providence.

Reading John's touching reflections on the inadequacies of intellectual understanding of creation's mysteries, I thought again of Vern, sitting in his living room surrounded by books and papers from contemporary theologians as he prepared to teach a Sunday-school lesson. John and Vern have made different choices about church membership, but both cherish their friendship with Russell and the role he played in their lives for more than twenty years. Each remains a thoughtful seeker and a devout believer, complete with doubts as well as theological lucidity.

Leadership's impact is leveraged when it is rooted in deep human connections. Beginning with the pastor's welcoming encounter with people, it is fostered in pastoral visits to home and hospital. It grows through the pastor's knocking on the doors of neighbors who have visited on Sunday or who live nearby, these strangers who might be open to a new relationship with Christ or Christ's body. It is extended through the establishment of small groups, formal and informal, where lives shared and love given and received become the sinews of a strong body and the arteries of faith's blood. Russell built the body of Faith Church upon such relationships over a period of many years, and the authenticity of those relationships helped bring into being the rich possibilities for people and parish that continue today.

chapter 4

Building Resilience

• *Christine* •

Christine had been pastor of First Church for nine years when the attack of pancreatitis landed her in the intensive-care unit, hooked up to IVs for five days. She's convinced that the strain this terrible illness put on her immune system contributed to the cervical cancer that suddenly appeared six months later, and may also have contributed to the appearance of a suspicious shadow that led to a second surgery a year after that. Her husband, William, was certain, with good medical reason, that she would die sometime during that awful five years of illness, four surgeries, and physical trauma. Meanwhile, the personal attacks and dysfunction at the church that had been waxing and waning for several years continued, at least in some quarters. It's no wonder that when Christine was strong enough again, she went off to the Southwest Career Center to examine whether she wanted to stay in ministry.

Her ministry didn't start out with such uncertainty, of course. Although as a young woman she didn't intend to go into ordained ministry at all, when she did "answer the call," she felt sure that this was the right path for her life. Her embrace of her vocation did not come quickly, however. While she had grown up in a church that she now looks back upon as a truly redemptive community, one where she was able to excel and become a leader, she never considered pastoral ministry a real possibility for a woman. So like countless other young people over the ages, she wandered away from church to find herself. But then, after a relationship crisis in college sent her into a spiral of searching that led her back to the church, followed by a time of exploring a career as a professional musician, she suddenly realized in the middle of a sermon by a minister—a woman!—that pastoral leadership was the work she felt called to do. So she enrolled in seminary and found herself both a believer and a success.

Christine came to First Church twenty years ago after a satisfy-ing first ministry in a family-size parish[1] in the Southeast. But she longed for a broader relationship with a larger group of staff col-leagues, so she began the search process that led to pleasing talks with the committee from First Church. Further investigation re-vealed that the climate—both meteorological and theological—of the Southwest was compatible with her delight in wide-open vistas and her liberal leanings, so she and William moved to begin a new adventure and to put down roots for a family.

Chuck and Tommie, longtime leaders at First Church, recall that Christine's preaching and worship leadership were terrific from the very beginning, and her public presence put her in good stead with many in the congregation. But some found her aloof (Chuck thinks she's just shy), and when she was confined to bed for the last couple of months of her pregnancy with Kevin, the church administrator moved into the power vacuum and tried to run the church. When Christine returned to work, the adminis-trator didn't want to let go, and so the struggles began that led Christine to conclude that the administrator had to be dismissed.

Christine recalls that dreadful period like this:

> Just take the worst elements of every story you've ever read about church conflict, and roll it all into one outrageous ball. Gossip, slander, side-group meetings, petitioned meetings, flyers, denominational officials who tried to be helpful but sometimes made it worse, stolen mailing lists, a thousand meetings, and a million phone calls. I am quite sure that if I had not had an infant at home who loved me unconditionally and needed me utterly, I would have quit or gone crazy.

At last about thirty-five people left the church to form a new congregation, but the script about Christine's being difficult to work with remained and kept popping up over the next ten years.

First Church had a history of difficult ministries. The district executive she talked with before accepting the call had told Christine, "Alcohol, divorce, depression, suicide, womanizing, laziness—you name it and it has happened among previous pastors here. . . . It's a strong church—it's had to be to get through everything it's gone through. But it's going to be a hard job. They may not really trust you or follow your lead for years."

In her youthful idealism, Christine didn't let this warning deter her, and she dived into the challenge of this new ministry with enthusiasm. She had read the literature that said ministers in larger churches, unlike the mom-and-pop parish from which she had come, had to be "in charge." So, despite her intent to be collaborative, she made decisions mostly through her own internal deliberations without sharing those processes with others. To outside observers, then, she seemed authoritarian and arbitrary. By the time the church administrator had to be fired, she had already asked the board to dismiss a music director who didn't want to follow the lead of this young woman, so her reputation as an autocrat was building.

These early battles caused her to be cautious, even frightened, of angry dynamics and hateful people. This newfound fearfulness led to a stage of passivity in making decisions, so when another administrator needed to be let go five years later, she lay low, hoping the elected leaders would act on their own. Finally, a breach of ethics had to be addressed, so once again she found herself the ogre. This episode led her to even greater discouragement, serious clinical depression, and doubt about her own gifts and call. When health problems laid her even lower, she was ready to leave—this church, if not ministry entirely.

Christine actually tried to leave First Church more than once. It was increasingly feeling to her like one of those institutional "clergy killers" that psychologist and church consultant Lloyd Rediger has described in his book bearing that title. But every time she felt like leaving, something in her own life—a baby born, cancer, a fruitless search process—held her there. What's more, the congregation, which could be so painfully combative, was also nurturing and generous to her when she was ill and during her pregnancy. Looking back over those years, she thinks the struggles alternating with the nurture conditioned her to begin thinking like a battered wife who hated her situation but couldn't find a way to leave. She had an abiding affection for the people, as many of them did for her, but the destructiveness was taking a terrible toll. Gradually, however, psychotherapy, Saint-John's-wort, her definition of firm new boundaries for herself, and a return to her spiritual roots began to turn the tide. Now she says simply, "God kept me here," and after twenty years as pastor of First Church, her staying does look like divine providence.

First Church is one of the fastest-growing congregations in its city and in its small denomination as well. It is unusual among such rapidly growing churches because it is quite liberal both theologically and socially—a "refuge church," as one consultant called it, providing safe harbor for its progressive members from the evangelical trend of late-twentieth-century society. Christine says they bumped up against the five-hundred-member barrier a couple of times before they took a giant leap of faith and called a second pastor, a decision that has opened the way to the present membership of eight hundred and worship attendance of about five hundred each Sunday. That risky move on the part of the church was one of the factors that changed the climate in the congregation and perhaps its character as well.

The greatest impetus for the congregation's growth, however, appears to have been Christine's increasing comfort in her role as the church's leader about ten years into her ministry there. Her settling in was prompted by three major changes she initiated at about that time in her life that made an enormous difference for her personally, and apparently for the church as well. First, she went to counseling, and in that supportive environment she began to learn some different ways of coping with the stress and new ways of bringing others along with her visionary ideas. Second, she went to a workshop on long-term pastorates led by Roy Oswald that helped her see how much fruitless energy is consumed by clergy moving from one congregation to another and how churches often thrive under long-term leadership. And third, she got reacquainted with God through a powerful mystical encounter that prompted her to begin to practice spiritual disciplines that nourished her.

Resources for resilience

Her ability to undertake these changes at all was a visible sign of Christine's innate resilience. Psychologists talk about resilience as the capacity to "bounce back" from difficult experiences, as well as the ability to endure challenging circumstances. The history of faith is rife with stories of resilient people. Israel's journey through enslavement, the wilderness, and countless struggles in the Promised Land display the resilience of a nation. When Paul writes that he has survived being beaten, imprisoned, and shipwrecked (see 2 Cor. 11:23–28 for the whole terrible list), and we place these hardships alongside the series of collegial and church conflicts he endured, it is clear that he had resilience.

More than thirty years ago, clinical psychologist Suzanne Kobasa coined the phrase "stress hardiness" to describe this personal resilience, basing her research on a group of business executives who endured a major restructuring of their company.[2] She found that three major traits contributed to hardiness among these executives: commitment, control, and challenge. By *commitment*, Kobasa meant people's involvement in activities that give them a sense of meaning and purpose and that heighten their motivation to achieve a goal. Embracing vocation is surely one significant way people express such commitment. Having a sense of internal *control*, rather than feeling at the mercy of outside forces, also makes an enormous difference for people as they are faced with difficulties. Viktor Frankl has described this attitude vividly in his reflections on surviving Auschwitz.[3] The Nazis might have been able to take away his freedom or even his life, but they could not take away his fundamental values or his search for meaning in the experiences of his life. Finally, responding to difficulties as a *challenge* rather than as a threat was a third fundamental trait of the stress-hardy executives. Hard times, rather than being viewed as blockades, are seen instead as an opportunity to exercise creativity.

Christine has demonstrated all three of these important traits in various ways. She thinks her ability to cope with those most difficult years of ministry is first of all rooted in having been reared in a family whose self-perception was "We don't cut bait; we keep fishing." She believes she was reasonably well nurtured as she was growing up, and included in that process was her parents' encouragement to stick with things, which led her to a determination to rise to challenges that confronted her in life.

What's more, Christine takes seriously her call and commitment to effective ministry and to the people she serves. While she understands clearly that she has not taken "life vows" to First Church, and in fact has at times actively explored leaving, she maintains a determination to be the best minister she can be and to serve the congregation as effectively as possible. She has made a deeply spiritual commitment and has treated that commitment with the faithfulness it deserves, especially as her own spiritual life has grown richer.

Christine's natural determination and her thoughtful demeanor allow her to exercise self-control fairly easily in many areas of her life. She's an introvert, first of all, so it comes naturally for her to think about responding before she speaks or acts. Furthermore, she learned to control her public presentation early in her training as a performance musician, so that she exhibited confidence, engaged the audience, and was able to express herself meaningfully, first with an oboe and later with words. (She remembers vividly her oboe teacher's making her practice repeatedly walking onstage to project herself to the audience, and many years later, she has lay leaders and pastoral interns do the same exercise as they practice walking to the pulpit.)

But her intellectualized approach to religion, characteristic of both her religious tradition and her active mind, began over time to lead her to believe that one's spiritual life could be contained and controlled like other aspects of life. Like many other parish pastors, Christine found herself becoming so attentive to the business of religion that she drifted away from the vitality of her personal faith—"away from everything I believed." As she began to recognize this tendency in herself, she started once again to engage in various spiritual practices, including meditation, spiritual reading, and centering prayer, and over a period of six months she had a series of full-blown mystical experiences. She recalls a line from Ntozake Shange's play, *For Colored Girls Who Have Considered Suicide / When the Rainbow Is Enuf,* that captured her experience well: "I found God in myself, and I loved her fiercely."

She especially recalls one evening during a clergy conference when the rest of the group went on a field trip to a famous church, but she instead went for a walk by the lake on the grounds of the retreat center where they were staying. She sat down by a statue on which was mounted a photo of a tiny infant cradled in the palm of a hand. The photo captured her attention and prompted her to borrow some votive candles from a nearby altar and arrange them around the picture. She quickly found herself entranced by the feeling of being held in that hand, becoming lost in the encounter until a clock struck the hour and she knew she had been in that liminal space for a full thirty minutes. Although she had planned to join her colleagues for a party later that evening, she stayed apart and savored the experience, folding it into her soul. And thus began a spiritual deepening that has vitalized her ministry ever since.

Her spiritual practices since that time have awakened in Christine an awareness of one of the great mysteries of faith. Just as Jesus reminded his followers that whoever would find life must lose it, so it is also true that faith by its very nature requires the relinquishment of certainty and control. As she has been enriched by the awareness of this truth, she has become more patient, grounded in expectant waiting while she has endured long periods of difficulty. Christine's deepening faith and active spiritual practice have become vital elements in her commitment to making this congregation a healthy and faithful community of caring and service. For Christine herself, faith and practice have strengthened her sense of being in control—not of the situations confronting her but of her responses to those challenges. She has come to realize that one is never really in control of things, and out of that recognition she embraces the Tao Te Ching's wisdom of stepping aside as a way of overcoming. The paradox of her faith is the fundamental paradox of all healthy faith: one gains control by letting go of control.

It is this awareness of her own inner locus of control and her commitment to trustful waiting that brings her to the central importance of forgiveness as an essential dimension of her practice of pastoral leadership. "You can collect a lot of hurts in this business," she observes about ministry, and as she recalls some of the hurtful things that were said and done in years past, she does sound remarkably understanding. She is aware, for example, that some of those who were so awful to her in those early years at First Church were mostly just skeptical of her youth and inexperience. Some of them have forgiven her, too, and now are active in the congregation. These changes remind her of a deathbed visit to a woman in her former parish with whom she'd had great conflict. As Christine came to visit this woman in her last hours of life, the woman told her of a dream she'd recently had of people from various parts of her life, including Christine, gathering at a Thanksgiving table—a vision of reconciliation as Christine sees it. "You know, Christine, we certainly did have our problems. You just needed to do it your own way," the woman said. And after a pause she added, "Well, keep on doing it." And then she died. Christine recalls that she and this woman had had some terrible fights over the years, and although they never really talked about those encounters, there was a forgiving reconnection in that moment that has taught Christine much about graceful ministry.

Ron, the congregation's assistant minister, sees Christine's firm grounding in faith as a principal reason for her effectiveness as a pastor. He knows very well that on her spiritual journey she has come through some difficult times to its present richness, and he observes, "You'll never taste the full sweetness of joy unless you've been through the depths of despair—and she has. We all go through tough stuff, and the only thing we can control is how we respond." Christine has learned that lesson well, and her continuing pattern of disciplined spiritual practices is an essential component of maintaining that awareness.

The "tough stuff" she has faced during her tenure at First Church appears to have heightened her resourcefulness and fostered her creativity in ministry. Over the years, as she has deepened her spirituality and recommitted herself to this ministry, she has met the challenges with new ideas and energy that have allowed the church, for example, to move beyond its five-hundred-member plateau and continue to grow. The church's increasing successes have reinforced her comfort with her own gifts and her own spiritual vitality, opening even more opportunities for her to share her extraordinary vision with the congregation in a transforming way.

Part of what has made this positive response to challenges possible is her reliance on personal support systems and her employment of appropriate coping mechanisms. Despite her natural shyness and introversion, Christine has made good use of various relationships to help sustain her through tough times. While she is grateful for the firm foundation her family provided in her early years, more recently she has drawn extra strength from a denominational clergy peer group and an interfaith spiritual sharing group. Both groups are the kinds of support systems that have been found to be important to the well-lived pastoral life. From time to time, she has also sought the specialized services of a psychotherapist and a spiritual director, and these days she contracts with a coach from the Alban Institute to guide her through new challenges as the church continues to develop. All of these relationships have no doubt contributed to her shedding the earlier reputation of being noncollaborative as she has learned to bring people along with her in change instead of telling them how they must change. She especially relishes her role in the church's decision to launch satellite congregations in underserved towns in her sparsely populated state because, although the idea was hers, she had to actively slow lay leaders down as they embraced and began to implement the plan. She wanted to be sure the whole congregation was on board.

Other coping strategies have been important to her as well. "I've always cultivated a hobby of some kind," she says. "It seems like a small thing, but there has been many a day when I retreated to a knitting project or my garden, in no small part to remind me that there was more to me than the currently tattered minister." Exercise, too, has been an essential part of her regimen, especially as she was rebuilding her strength after that long period of illnesses. And she takes every opportunity she can to participate in formal and informal professional education experiences to be the continuous learner she strives to be.

SEEKING THE BEST RESOURCES—FROM ANY SOURCE

It took eighteen months for Dewey, the founding pastor of Sandia Church, to assemble the core group of forty people who were meeting regularly in the school gymnasium when they launched the new congregation in 1990. Then one Sunday they went from 40 to 320 in attendance, the surge prompted primarily by a telemarketing campaign coupled with mailings and personal calls. Dewey quickly points out, "We just beat the advent of answering machines, voice mail, and cell phones" that would stifle such an approach today. But nontraditional strategies to building and being church have characterized the congregation's life as it has continued to grow to its present fifteen hundred members. "The church development person on our denomination's national staff told me that every new church that was rapidly growing had been accused of not being denominational enough," he says, and Dewey has heard the complaints about Sandia Church as well. But in the twenty years he served as pastor, Dewey was always looking for the best resources for fostering growth in the church, regardless of the source.

Resilient Leadership

Christine's resilience is a cornerstone of her effective leadership. A central dimension of this resilience has been learning to adapt her approach in the face of the challenges she and the congregation have faced together. David, the retired dean of the school of education at the local university, finds Christine's leadership a "fascinating" case study in situational leadership, a concept and skill he taught enthusiastically during his career. Again and again, she has modified the manner in which she has conducted her ministry, making adjustments in the face of changing circumstances. As church membership has grown, for example, she has learned to deal more indirectly with the congregation, helping other staff members figure out what they can do. And when rituals like sharing joys and concerns that worked well in a smaller congregation became cumbersome for the growing church, she and the liturgy committee together found ways to adapt the treasured practice. Her adjustments and the church's adjustments unfolded in harmony.

From his perspective as both an academic administrator and a former member of the church board, David is impressed with the church's "pretty smooth operation these days." He sees this smoothness as the direct result of Christine's having adapted her ministry in the face of those earlier troubled times, always finding new ways of engaging with congregational leaders to respond to emerging opportunities for growth and service. He cites the way Christine and the congregation have dealt with the physical plant, for example, as a mark of her evolving leadership ability. Not only is she persistent in working toward addressing needs, like overseeing the addition of a religious-education building for growing numbers of children in the church, but she also works collaboratively with both staff and lay leaders with the attitude, "Let's design it together." He knows she had a reputation as being a bit authoritarian in years past, but he sees no sign of that now and believes that this change is another example of the positive results of her situational leadership.

David thinks Christine is "Wheatley-like," referring to Margaret Wheatley, organizational consultant and author of the influential book *Leadership and the New Science*. Wheatley draws on the language of quantum physics to describe attributes of effective leadership as they emerge and change in the context of particular relationships and circumstances. She argues that understanding the quantum world is key because "All life participates actively with its environment in the process of coadaptation and coevolution. No sub-atomic particle exists independent of its participation with other particles."[4] When Christine came to First Church, her expectation of herself as a leader, based upon her reading of

church leadership theory and despite her natural inclination toward collaboration, was that she must be firmly managerial and
carry the burden of being the principal visionary in the congregation. Perhaps this impulse was driven in part by her youthful
idealism. It may also have been, at least in some small measure,
the result of pressure widely recognized by the first generation of
mainline women pastors, who felt especially pressured to perform
and prove their strength. Or maybe it was just the perfect storm of
a new pastor's immersion in a complicated and difficult system, as
the district executive had warned. Whatever the contributing factors, Christine's particle engaged with the system of particles that
made up First Church in a way that fostered a powerful tension
that was not easily resolved. While that tension could ultimately
have led to division or even destruction of one or the other, the energy was ultimately channeled into creativity that has now become
the "pretty smooth operation" called First Church.

David also thinks of Christine and the church as a jazz band,
playing not from a predetermined score but from cues given to
each other, and he wonders if this approach might be rooted in
her early career as a musician. But he says that when she is in the
pulpit, "She is simultaneously responding to what she sees in our
reaction to what she is saying and to the text that she intended to
present." So he sees her most often as not "talking to" but "working with." The resulting smoothness may be significantly related to
Christine's spiritual foundation, which David sees displayed in her
serenity. "I've never seen her scowl or heard in her voice the kind
of tension that I would feel. Her equanimity conveys an openness
that says, 'If you have troubles, you can talk to me. I'll listen.'"
And that openness also manifests in the way she encourages others or engages in dialogue with those who might disagree with her.
When he asks her what she thinks about an issue, for instance, he
sees her respond quite honestly, but only to a certain point, as if to
avoid telling him what he should think. David sees this authentic
and respectful self-presentation evident in her preaching as well,
demonstrating "her capacity to talk with the congregation about
what she believes, while somehow inviting others to do their own
thinking as well."

Transforming the bricks

Christine doesn't dream about leaving First Church any more, at least not until she retires in a few years. Fantasies of escaping from the misery have disappeared because—well, the misery has disappeared. Besides, she finds too much that interests her in her current ministry. But she's cautious about predicting how much lasting influence she will have had on the church. She believes that some programs started during her tenure will probably last, like the satellite congregations in other communities, because that successful program has become a model for other churches. But she learned when she left her first parish that when you leave, you lose whatever control you may have had, and your influence is all in the past. It endures only "in the bricks," as one of that church's matriarchs put it. "Still," she adds, "I'd like to think that I've been here long enough that what was in the bricks when I came—'the minister is going to betray us'—is gone." David conjectures that Christine probably doesn't think about having some enduring impact because "she has her hands full thinking about *right now*," and she and the church both live vigorously in the present moment.

Chrstine clearly hopes, and I think with good reason, that her long ministry has been a time of cleansing. The "stress hardiness" that she has displayed seems newly embedded in the life of this "pretty smooth operation," and the confidence and hope evident in those who are part of the church these days seem to be strong mortar for sustaining the bricks. Christine's resilience seems infectious, as the operations and even the very bricks of First Church also seem more resilient.

With a "Wheatley-esque" perspective, Christine shared with me a story about literally examining the church's bricks and making a surprising discovery. It was a quiet Friday when she walked around the building, looking particularly at the bricks in the walls. She remembers the stains and scars of those fifty-year-old walls, but she also noticed the strength and durability she saw there. As she took in her surroundings, she thought of the ways in which she herself was like those walls, both scarred and durable.

As I looked around the sanctuary, I noticed that the mural is fading and peeling. If the congregational craziness is in the bricks, the congregational health is in this mural. It's kept this congregation centered in its religious values all these years. I think that someone entering this room for the first time would sense a lively congregation here, and would probably understand something of who we are just by looking around. It's a good room.

What came to me, sitting a while in that quiet space, was that I, too, am frayed and flawed; that in particular, I played my part in each of these crises that have caused us such pain—acted or became passive in anger or anxiety or hurt or sheer bewilderment. I neglected to do some hard things I might have done, let some things happen that I probably should have stuck my neck out to stop, didn't take some risks that would have probably paid off.

I have thought these things before, and even said some of them to others, when it was obvious that this was what was expected of me, but this time they felt real—sunken in. I realized with a start that someday—maybe even already—somebody is going to be exasperated by what's "in the bricks," and what's "in the bricks" is going to be—among other things—me.

Long-time chuch members Chuck and Tommie think a number of fruits of her ministry will endure after Christine leaves someday—besides the satellite congregations in nearby towns. They point to the "welcoming congregation" initiative that extends hospitality to everyone who comes to the church, regardless of race, gender, sexual orientation, or economic circumstances. And they believe the organizational structure that has evolved as the church has grown will likely be lasting. They are sure that she will be missed and that her departure will be a big loss, but the church will go on as it has for the thirty years they have been part of First Church. Ron thinks Christine's commitment to experiment and change has set a lasting pattern for the church's life and ministry, "not to get it perfectly, but to do it, adjust, and move on." First Church will continue to be a creation in progress, always adapting to the new situations in which it finds itself.

Christine says her central desire has been to build a healthier community, and it certainly appears that she is successful in that aim. She hopes that the best contribution of her ministry will be found in the spiritual depth that has blossomed during her tenure and that this essential aspect of the church's health will endure long after she has become a distant memory. She puts her belief this way: "Taking spiritual risks and being the carrier of depth and meaning and thirst into whatever we are doing, invoking and evoking the holy in the service of healing and transformation are the very heart of our calling as ministers."

It's clear to me that what is now in the bricks is Christine's resilience, held together by her tears, her deep connection with Mystery, her unflinching dedication to truth, her rootedness in community, and her daring to hope in the future. All these are intermingled with the congregation's willingness to cooperate in its own transformation under her leadership. The members have not been passive in that process—not by a long shot. But through her example and her prodding, the congregation, too, has claimed more deeply the trio of factors—commitment, control, and challenge—that constitute hardiness. Call it faith, if you like.

chapter 5

Passion for Justice

• *Trey* •

Trey offers a quiet "thank you" as I pay for the coffee at Flying Star, our community's favorite meeting spot. "I got stripped of all my cash yesterday from people coming by the church needing help," he explains apologetically. Trey has for ten years been pastor of La Mesa Church, a small but vibrant congregation located in what is now dubbed the International District of the city. The neighborhood used to be called "the War Zone" in the press because of the frequent crime and the drug, prostitution, and gang activity that still occur in the area, where nearly a third of the fifteen thousand residents live below the federal poverty level. But people in the area have begun to fight back against the negative social forces and the disparaging reputation, and they have begun to trumpet their pride in the rich ethnic diversity that has been brought to their neighborhood by immigrants from many cultures, including not a few undocumented. La Mesa Church has been increasingly involved in this transformation, and Trey's determined leadership has been at the forefront of bringing some of those changes into reality.

La Mesa Church looks like thousands of other urban congregations in changing neighborhoods across the country—congregations composed predominantly of older people of European descent worshiping in aging buildings that are beginning, despite some refurbishing over the years, to feel drab and cavernous on Sunday mornings. The church is three blocks from the state fairgrounds and two blocks north of old Route 66, where 1950s-era motels that once offered overnight hospitality to families on the road now provide transient housing for near-homeless families, or rent rooms by the hour for less wholesome activity. The elementary school across the street from the church has had a student turnover rate of more than 100 percent for each of the past several years. Mexican and other Latin American immigrants are the largest group of students, and when walking the hallways of the school or the sidewalks outside, one is more likely to hear Spanish than English spoken. But the neighborhood's colorful Buddhist Temple and Talin Market, a sprawling ethnic grocery owned by a Vietnamese family and boasting rich delicacies from all over the world, attest to the strong influx of newcomers from several Asian countries. And when the men's African drumming group occasionally beats a jubilant welcome before La Mesa's Sunday worship services, the presence of the Somali refugee community is evident. The International District is a lively neighborhood facing many difficult challenges, and La Mesa Church stands right in the middle of it all.

Trey was on his denomination's national staff, guiding the church's work in urban ministries, when he concluded, "I'm really a pastor at heart." He yearned to lead a local community of faith and to work once again at the grass roots for change. He describes his national service as sort of a midcareer second seminary education where he "came to understand the truth of Loren Mead's analysis that we are in the midst of a breakdown of the old paradigm for being church." So he began to look for a call to a congregation where he could be on the front lines of those changes. "La Mesa is exactly that kind of church, reinventing itself as it moves from its programmatic past to being more relational while building on a rich fifty-year heritage of service," he says proudly. "Now the future is wide open. The best years of La Mesa's life are ahead of us." Note the "us"!

Trey has been an ordained minister all his adult life, entering a denominational seminary right out of college. He had been shaped by the climate of the 1960s and 1970s, when radical social changes were unfolding in society and the church was guiding many of those changes. He had not grown up in a religious home, although his mother was quite progressive socially. But as a teenager he had a sense that something was missing from his life, so he began attending church with a friend. There he was influenced by the pastor's preaching and teaching about social justice, and he remembers being especially impressed by the life and ministry of Martin Luther King Jr. "I thought Dr. King offered a powerfully prophetic voice for God's intentions for America," he recalls. The lure of working toward a more just society and his admiration for the church's leadership in the movements of those days caused him to shift from his initial study of physics to preparing for ministry, and he went off to seminary in 1975.

Clear focus

It was during those seminary years that Trey began making some fundamental decisions about the impact he hoped to make in his ministry. First and most important, he began to say that he wanted "to advance the reign of Christ on earth." For Trey, that meant that he needed to concentrate his time and energies on two parallel goals: promoting social justice and taking the long view—"the view of the grandmother," as he calls it. His "grandmotherly" approach required a welcoming, compassionate spirit and a persistent dedication to working over time on targeted critical issues that he defined as practical manifestations of the justice necessary for Christ's reign on earth.

So during seminary and continuing from his first pastorates in urban congregations to today, he has focused his work on several major issues. The first of these was the growing scourge of homelessness that was just becoming more visible in the early 1980s. This passion has led him to found three separate homeless shelters over the course of ministry in four urban congregations, including La Mesa. He has also served as president of the board of a non-profit housing corporation that sought to find permanent homes for homeless people. During one of his previous ministries, he served as president of the board of an affordable housing nonprofit group that renovated a blighted slum property into a successful mixed-income community of four hundred apartments. In recent years he was the founding president of the local Opportunity Center, which provides a pathway out of homelessness for seventy-four men each night, and people from the La Mesa congregation have been deeply involved in this work.

A second focus of his nearly thirty years of ministry has been to relieve hunger. Besides expanding his church's food pantry, which is open seven days a week ("People need to get food whenever they are hungry," one of his church members recalls his emphasizing), he has served on the national board of Heifer International to address hunger internationally and on the board of his denomination's hunger program as well. Besides these practical responses of providing food for hungry mouths, he has also worked on more systemic issues like food-stamp reform and access. Trey takes quite literally Jesus's command to "feed my sheep," and he applies that command to the modern structures of society.

His third major emphasis, and his approach to addressing these justice issues over the years, has been community organizing. He has supplemented his theological perspective with the operating principles of Saul Alinsky and others, an approach he considers one of the most significant social movements of the twentieth century. This interest led him to become involved with the fledgling Community Interfaith, a ministry that he was delighted to discover when he began his work at La Mesa. He has since served as cochair of Community Interfaith and has become well known, though not always with appreciation, by most of the political leaders of the city as a result of this community organization's work of bringing the values of certain institutions—churches, schools, unions, and nonprofits—into public life.

Mary Lou was on the pastoral search committee that recommended calling Trey to La Mesa Church. She's been a member of the congregation for twenty-five years and recalls with gratitude the last long-term minister, Howard, who led the congregation in deciding to stay and serve in its changing neighborhood. A series of short-term and interim ministers between Howard and Trey sapped some of the church's confidence, and when the search committee interviewed Trey, its members were attracted to the fact that "he was very certain of his grounding, his view of what is important, what the church needs to be." Trey's passion for social justice and commitment to making a difference in the lives of people and the community as a whole were exactly what they wanted. "We waited a long time for Trey's response to our invitation to come be our pastor, but when he says yes, he means it." There's that persistence again.

David, the church's longtime choir director, recalls that when Trey came to La Mesa, he joined a succession of pastors who all had a commitment to working in the neighborhood. But he noticed that Trey brought a specific commitment to immersing himself in the demands of urban ministry in a way that energized the congregation. Somehow his hands-on approach allowed the congregants to recast their vision of being church in concrete ways. He remembers, for example, Trey's befriending a police officer in those early months and finagling an invitation to ride patrol with the officer to become more familiar with the neighborhood. Trey's rides with the patrolman opened his eyes, and through his stories in sermons and conversations with others, opened the eyes of many in the congregation to the real life and pressing needs of the church's incredibly diverse neighbors.

Before Trey came to La Mesa, the church had institutionalized its outreach to the neighborhood, responding to the needy with referrals to government programs and social-service agencies. Trey insisted that the people in the congregation "get more relational," dealing directly with the people around them. They had to learn to be "good neighbors" in very practical ways. Trey insisted they put away the list of agencies to which they could refer the needy who appeared at the church's door, at least as a first response, and begin to speak and work directly with these neighbors. Trey was himself often the first contact, but he quickly recruited and trained others to join him in being available to those in need. He persuaded the church to create a "Samaritan Fund" that he could draw upon for immediate help, but he also insisted on talking with the people who appeared for help to explore possibilities for their futures. He was determined to help them look beyond immediate, tangible assistance and to plan for and take practical steps to improve their situations.

The fruitfulness of his ministry over the years, and the high regard in which people hold him, emerges first of all from his self-differentiated recognition of the importance of working for social justice, which was born in his adolescence, fired during his seminary years, and refined over the years of his ministry. This commitment has become the heart of his pastoral identity as he lives out his persistent commitments. Further, his own priorities do not keep him from appreciating the needs and perspectives of others, especially those for whom he is called to be pastor. The freedom to extend the church's ministry into the larger community happens "because Trey does his pastoral work in the church," says Judy, one of the church's elders.

Trey's clarity extends also to his awareness of the geographical place in which he finds himself. In fact, he once wrote a study guide for a book that spells out the implications of a "theology of place."[1] In his writing and in his day-to-day ministry, he makes evident his belief that God is the "placer" of congregations and ministers and that our task is to serve the reign of Christ and incarnate community *where we are.* In this theology of place, he emphasizes that being placed in a particular locale does not limit ministry but can in fact stimulate a deeper, more significant impact of one's work. The boundaries of location contain one's focus, he believes, as a nozzle on a garden hose focuses the flow of water for greater power.

Trey attributes his clarity of purpose to three mentors in his lifelong education. Carl, one of his seminary professors, first acquainted him with the biblical and theological teachings that call people of faith to commit themselves to working for justice in the world. Phil, a fellow student in seminary who went on to serve as a parish pastor and on the national staff of their denomination, has been a peer support for Trey for thirty years, and they have been enlivened by working together in common efforts around community organizing, community development, and affordable housing.

George, another early mentor and longtime friend, taught Trey the practicalities of a justice-focused life out of his own long years of laboring in urban parishes and then national and international leadership posts. George lived in "commitment to the coming reign of Christ," as Trey once wrote about him. Jim, Trey's judicatory executive, believes that this friendship with George over the years has been a primary sustaining force for Trey's durability through the challenges of effective urban ministry.

Trey's clarity about who he is, where he is called to be, and the central focus of his ministry are keys to the impact of his leadership. Mary Lou and the search committee sensed this clarity in what they called "the certainty of his grounding." It is clear when one talks with Trey that this certainty is not in any way rigid or self-righteous, although some of La Mesa's members have noted that he can occasionally be a little too controlling about the minutiae. They recall, for example, the time he took down the blue Advent banners the committee had put up the night before, because they did not fit his aesthetic assessment of the sanctuary. He can be, as Mary Lou says, a bit of a perfectionist, although this trait could be seen as part of the high bar he sets for himself and for the church in being faithful to God's call. But she also thinks he is blessed to serve in a church with folk who can be exceedingly deferential and forgiving because they respect his passion and his hard work. Clarity of focus is, after all, nurtured in a supportive community.

A LIFELONG COMMITMENT TO RENEWAL

"I would hope that the vision of our parish, as a post–Vatican II parish, is calling people forth to ecumenism, evangelization, and justice and charity," Joel says in looking back on his twenty-five-year ministry at Holy Rosary parish. "Most of all, we built it together with the people. We have a collegial model here." Joel and his parish leaders have just completed writing a pastoral plan for the years ahead, a process timed to correspond with his retirement as pastor in the next few months. Joel's spirit is very much a part of that collaboratively developed plan, and his lifelong commitment to church renewal is much in evidence. Joel was ordained during the years of the Second Vatican Council, and his entire ministry has displayed a central thread of empowering the laity to implement that "new vision of Catholicism" that he eagerly embraced as a young priest. He finds that this trend is not much in favor in the larger church these days, but his deeply held commitment to that vision has shaped the life and ministry of Holy Rosary parish in ways that seem certain to endure.

Christ's reign

Embracing the clarity of the prophet Micah, Trey believes that God's reign requires people "to do justice, and to love kindness, and to walk humbly with your God" (Micah 6:8). He applies these prophetic words in a variety of ways in his life. In 2007, for example, he honored George, his mentor, by nominating him and his wife, Kathy, for a national award given by their denomination for a lifetime of outstanding contributions to social-justice ministries. In his speech introducing them for the presentation, Trey quoted from one of George and Kathy's Christmas letters to illustrate their commitments:

> This is the joy and hope of Christmas, that God in person joins humanity as the child of a poor couple. He shatters chaos. He shows in his humility, his healing, his neighborliness, his anger against oppression, his teaching, and his sacrificial living what the human possibilities are. Through this action of God in the life of his people, a way is open to us to join God in overcoming hopelessness and disorder, and in realizing a New World of peace with justice.

These words, Trey said, convey a profound understanding of "the reign of Christ" that Trey believes the church is called to embrace, and the vision they convey is the foundation of his ministry.

Undergirding the lofty language, Trey's implementation of this vision in his own ministry is focused on the nitty-gritty practicalities of this world. He recalls the words of one of his colleagues in urban ministry who confessed to getting a little weary of his liberal friends always taking the systemic view: "When a man needs a Band-Aid, for goodness sakes, give him a Band-Aid." Or as his mentor Saul Alinsky put it in his classic book, "Tactics means doing what you can with what you have."[2] Trey seeks both mercy and justice in his ministry. He is as committed to providing food for and nurturing a relationship with the hungry neighbor who appears at La Mesa's door as he is to changing civic policy by giving an impassioned speech at a city council meeting favoring better working conditions for bus drivers.

Trey has recognized throughout his ministry that his work for Christ's reign must not be done in isolation. In fact, the very nature of collaborative effort in the pursuit of justice is itself a fundamental manifestation of Christ's incarnate reign. So he has devoted himself to work not only in and with his parish, but also with networks of secular and parachurch organizations and informal groups that share his concerns. His longtime friend and colleague Phil recalls with admiration the national urban ministry conference Trey organized ten years ago that fostered this sense of shared ministry. "It was not a dog-and-pony show of speeches," Phil says, "but a laboratory-learning approach that allowed participants to engage in hands-on ways with local congregations and projects." The action-reflection learning model upon which the conference was based provided opportunity for participants to come together, and later to stay in touch, as they shared new ideas about doing urban ministry while at the same time strengthening their support systems. "Trey is always neck-deep in the work himself, but is also always inviting people to both act and reflect on their actions," Phil adds.

On a local level, Trey's engagement with Community Interfaith has not only expanded his impact on local issues; it has also built community and touched the lives of individuals in transformative ways. Kip, executive of Community Interfaith, joined La Mesa Church precisely because of Trey's clarity and balance, which he sees displayed in the life of the congregation as a whole. Kip grew up in a decidedly nonreligious home, and his "fancy education" (Princeton, Oxford, Stanford) led him to an academic life on the faculty of the local law school. But three years ago, he became acquainted with the work of Community Interfaith through his interest in working on social-justice issues in the community. He got to know Trey through those encounters, and his growing respect for Trey's leadership led him to begin attending La Mesa Church. Finally, a year ago, he resigned from the law-school faculty to take a job on the payroll of Community Interfaith.

"It was not until I became acquainted with Trey through Community Interfaith that I came to see the religious basis for a commitment to social justice," Kip tells me. "I started reading Walter Brueggemann's *Hope within History* and began to see the depth of what I had been missing. My colleagues at the law school were speechless when I told them what I was going to do." La Mesa Church, which Kip now attends regularly, was central to his transition into work with Community Interfaith, and he sums up his appreciation for Trey like this:

> He's patient. He needles and agitates me periodically, and still lets me sort things out in my own time. I'm coming to an understanding of what it means to be a Christian; I've felt very welcomed at that table. Trey has created a culture of relationship, of caring for each other and for the community as a whole.

Trey fosters this culture of deep caring by his own attitude about his pastoral work. "It's such a privilege," he says, "to be given access to people's lives at vulnerable times." Again, the reign of Christ is not just about social action for justice, but it is necessarily also about warm and nurturing personal relationships. Christ's good news is conveyed in the context of warmly human relationship addressing vexing social issues.

Jim points out that Trey clearly understands that the power of institutions in people's lives extends beyond just relationships. The effective quest for justice and the pursuit of God's reign has become, in this complicated world, a necessarily organizational task. Trey demonstrates this understanding, he says, not only in his work to challenge the larger institutions of society to be more just, but also in his engagement with the judicatory. Jim explains:

Trey . . . [carefully] picks his work in the larger church to be able to extend his core mission commitments. He's been involved, for example, on the new-church development committee in order to help launch an immigrant parish on the west side of town. His investments are always visionary, sometimes at the cost of the necessary practical implementation of ideas.

Despite his recognition of the importance of organizations and institutions in pursuing God's reign on earth, Trey's greatest weakness as a pastor may be his limitations as an administrator. Jim notes, "Administration is not Trey's long suit, but especially gifted people may need to be surrounded by thick-skinned administrators who take up the mundane matters of institutions." Since La Mesa is a smaller congregation, that detail work is most often done by those forgiving laypeople Mary Lou mentioned. Trey might respond, though, that "the coming reign of Christ" is always unfolding, always incomplete, so the practical details of bringing that reign into being must always be in formation. As the poet Longfellow said in his poem "Retribution," "the mills of God grind slowly, yet they grind exceeding small." Or maybe understanding this area in Trey's life could be simply a matter of recognizing his strong "P" (Perceiving) score on the Myers-Briggs Type Indicator that underlies his creative nature while also shaping his occasionally frustrating administrative style. (But Trey's peripatetic ministry might also provoke an observer to wonder whether Jesus may also have been a "P" on the MBTI.)

Grandmotherly care

It certainly took some patience and gradual work for La Mesa Church to realize a dream that Trey had planted and that the congregation had nurtured for several years. Three years ago Judith was called to the staff to begin a ministry with Native American people in the neighborhood. A child of two Native American tribes, Judith had served in several ecumenical and denominational ministries, but like Trey, she felt called to focus her work in a specific place. She was drawn to La Mesa because the congregation under Trey's leadership seemed to hold "a deep desire to explore what God might be doing among Native peoples." She has found the church to be genuinely interested in learning about Native people's cultures, and she has mostly appreciated Trey's nondirective style and openness to her ministry, which has emerged as quite broad and not too closely tied to the congregation. He shows his support and guides her work primarily by asking questions about what she is discovering, what is emerging in her work, what she has acted on, and what her next steps might be. "He is respectful of my culture and our differences, including gender, and celebrates the diversity of our work as a rich part of God's complex world."

When asked what she wishes Trey did better as a pastoral leader, Judith declines to identify any frustrations or wish for changes. She points out, "Our cultural tradition is to accept whatever life gives you as a lesson. It is what it is. The task is always to work with what is." In her acceptance, Judith shares one key aspect of Trey's leadership—they both begin with a radical acceptance of the realities they face, and they both engage those challenges with patient persistence growing out of their fundamental values and commitments.

His instinctive patience is probably one reason Trey has become a good fly fisherman. David, La Mesa's choir director, who has become a good friend, introduced him to the sport a month after Trey arrived at the church, and Trey has now become something of a fanatic about it. Standing in an icy mountain stream, he says, confirms the necessity of suffering and deprivation while at the same time renewing his determination to endure and to hope. He's inspired by the fishing tales from John Gierach's book *Dances with Trout* to bring a unique perspective to the necessity of patience in all of life. "I have not caught a salmon in three years, and I am still giving it a go" must be the attitude one brings to the task, he insists. Ministry, like fly-fishing, can sometimes be profoundly frustrating, and the only appropriate antidote is patience—"the very nature of God," as the church father Tertullian put it.

Trey insists, however, that the patience of a Christian leader must be balanced by action that changes the world as it is encountered. "The itch for justice and mercy always demands scratching," he says. This task began in his current ministry by first addressing the culture of La Mesa itself—specifically the parsimony he confronted when he arrived. "When he came, we thought we were poor," Mary Lou recalls. "We were always on the edge financially. But Trey operates from a theology of abundance—that we must believe in God's abundance. He believes there will always be a way for what God wishes to be carried out." The tightfistedness Trey encountered at La Mesa may have been a byproduct of an incident forty years earlier when the church's treasurer embezzled some money. Or it may be simply the result of many years of gradually declining membership that fostered a creeping insecurity before Trey arrived.

Trey remembers those early struggles about money and recalls the frequent complaints that "we don't have the money." He would counter by saying that money is never the limiting resource, only lack of commitment. If the commitment is there, the money will come, because God is resourceful. He pointed out that budgets are moral documents and that this is as true for a congregation or a family as it is for a city. Just as cities must take care of employees and neighborhoods, so congregations must generously care for the world they serve. Trey is a powerful preacher, and his persistent proclamation of God's abundance and the demand for generosity eventually transformed La Mesa's self-image. The congregation now hosts a counseling center, a neighborhood after-school arts program, and a food pantry, and its building calendar is bursting with countless community meetings and frequent neighborhood gatherings. It turns out, as Trey promised the members, that they can do it all—or at least a lot.

Jim sees the change in attitude about money that Trey brought to the congregation as a fundamental transformation for the church that set in motion much of La Mesa's subsequent mission. "It took three years, but they now operate like there is more money here than they need, and they can do whatever they choose to do," he says. Pastoral leadership, it seems, is a lot like being a community organizer—and it's a real job with actual responsibilities!

David shares the perception that Trey's patiently persistent leadership has transformed the congregation itself. "La Mesa never reaches a point of stasis," he says. "With Trey, it's always, 'Let's try this.' The congregation is always pushing the boundaries, trying to get back to what the church is called to be, making a difference in society, not being an insular club." Trey motivates people, David says, "by building them up, recognizing the good stuff they do. He's absolutely unafraid to confront issues that must be addressed; he doesn't let things fester. But he generally approaches things in a positive way that balances needs as he sees them." Trey's "loving grandmother" approach makes him a positively persuasive prophet.

Jim believes that Trey's attempt to guide La Mesa into becoming a more diverse, multiethnic congregation has not yet borne full fruit. He wonders whether Trey might be a bit reluctant to confront the old culture with the need for new ways of doing things—especially in worship, where the style is still very much rooted in the traditions of their denomination. David believes that this reluctance grows out of Trey's concern not to alienate older members of the congregation as change is happening in other arenas of congregational life. Like a good pastoral psychotherapist, Trey respects the defenses of the people in his parish and surrounds them with unconditional positive regard, even as he searches for the key to their motivation for change. The fiery prophet at the city council meeting becomes the gentle pastor back home in the church, inviting and coaxing and encouraging new life to emerge in its own time. Trey himself is clear that the congregation is changing its liturgical practices at an appropriate pace, in keeping with both its traditions and its multicultural context. "We have world music, Native drumming, a Hispanic children's dance troupe, a Kid's Club choir that looks like the United Nations." He points out that these changes are symbols of the diversity of the neighborhood and signs of La Mesa's transformation, even as they are grounded in the traditions the congregation has inherited.

Who knows, really, how quickly change should come? Transforming society, like being a loving grandmother, is not an overnight process or a change accomplished through a single encounter in time. Trey understands that the community organizing Saul Alinsky taught is consistent with the life Jesus lived and the vision Jesus offered. Trey's background has helped him see that working for justice requires more than just taking to the streets or radically confronting civic or religious assemblies, although these clamorous encounters are sometimes necessary. But transformation is more often a slow, patient process that works to change the system from within, penetrating such institutions as churches, unions, neighborhood organizations, city councils, and political parties. Despite his passionate commitment to justice, Trey remains a loving pastor who recognizes that change is not easy for people. So he continually balances a patient trust in God with an activist determination to usher in the reign of Christ.

Pursuit of bliss

Trey's quest for balance in his ministry also extends to his life beyond the formal parameters of his work. That's one big reason he has embraced fly-fishing so completely. In an essay relating this avocation to his vocation as minister, Trey cites Joseph Campbell's words from his book *Pathways to Bliss*: "But I do know what bliss is, that deep sense of being present, of doing what you absolutely must do to be yourself. If you can hang onto that, you are on the edge of the transcendent already."[3] Trey's passion for justice, lived out in his ministry at La Mesa Church, brings as much bliss to his heart as spending a crisp autumn day on the river casting for trout. This joy that he finds in pursuing his high calling—"I love this work," he exclaims—is part of what sustains him, and it is central to the leadership he offers the parish. Phil agrees that it is Trey's clarity and the depth of his sense of call that sustains him. "The ones who burn out are the ones who are struggling with their call. I never hear of the committed ones burning out."

Maintaining enthusiasm for ministry can be a challenge for all clergy, and perhaps especially for those like Trey who are so engaged in the struggle for justice. Nurturing relationships are one of the components of Trey's support system. Jim thinks Trey's long friendship with his mentor, George, is an attachment that keeps him centered and committed to his call. Since he's been at La Mesa, Trey has also come to cherish his friendship with David, especially their shared devotion to fly-fishing. And he's had some long-term relationships over the years in which he has found comfort and encouragement. But he says, "I've never found clergy groups all that helpful to me. Community-organizing groups, on the other hand, engage me with all kinds of people. Maybe I'm just kind of a reluctant clergyman, a contrarian, and I struggle with that formal professional identity as a minister."

Nevertheless, he is disciplined about daily prayer and particularly values the Celtic branch of Christianity, which impels him to seek the "thin places" of life. He makes a silent retreat occasionally to allow himself time to read and think and pray. And, of course, there is the fishing, the time in nature that is restorative and re-energizing. "Earlier in my life I did not understand the importance of balance between work and non-work," he says. "Now I've found that effective ministry requires saying no to some things that might become unnecessary burdens and yes to some things that bring joy. I like balance better."

Trey is comfortable in his introverted skin, and he is content to withdraw at the end of a long day of pastoral engagement to read and think and restore his energies. His life and effectiveness in ministry are a ringing affirmative response to Presbyterian minister Adam McHugh's question in a *Christian Century* article, "Can Introverts Lead?"[4] Despite his skills as a preacher and the passion of his beliefs, Trey is not a charismatic figure who draws adoring followers to his cause. He is more like the humble Level 5 leader whom Jim Collins extols in his book *Good to Great*. He thinks before he acts, and he reflects carefully on the consequences of his behavior before he takes his next steps. He builds trust, Judy says, by listening to people's stories and telling some of his own. And because he is able to weave those stories and thoughtful reflections into powerful visions for the future, he is also attracting a new generation of leaders like Kip who can extend God's reign even further.

"Good leaders attract good followers," Jim says, "and it's not yet clear to me that the new followers that Trey is attracting are committed to the church's work as much as they are drawn to Trey's leadership. At some point a leader must convert *my* work into *our* work." But Trey is confident that the leadership base in the congregation is broadening well. "My job as a pastor is not to build a ministry around me but to build leaders. Any good pastor or organizer gets that." To that end he reminds the parishioners whenever a new member joins, they are now a different community that needs to stretch to embrace everyone's interests, gifts, and commitments.

He anticipates that all who join will take their places in the leadership of the community. "I sometimes liken a congregation to a tanker that has momentum and a direction you need to understand before you attempt to steer it differently," he says. "As a pastor it is good to stay long enough to understand where that tanker has been, where God might want it to be going, and how you can get as many as possible on the bridge to make that happen."

Judy is confident that Trey "will have fostered a commitment of God's people here in this neighborhood to be at work in the world, so that faith makes a difference. It may take a variety of shapes and speak different languages, but it will endure." Phil believes that "when Trey does leave La Mesa, I don't think people will leave when a new minister comes, because I think people are committed to the mission of La Mesa to the community." Mary Lou adds that one specific way this change will continue is that La Mesa will never "go back to being a big empty shell that only gets opened on Sundays. Trey has made this a church that will never be content again to sit on its can."

David goes further to suggest that someday people will say that Trey was prophetic because he recognized the need for the church to change to respond to the times, and because he attracted and trained the leaders to accomplish needed changes. "Our denomination is declining," David observes, "but Trey's vision and energy and creativity are allowing us to do a new thing in the world. And thank God it's drawing new people like Kip into the work we share."

Kip thinks Trey's long-term impact goes far beyond the perimeter of the church itself. "The city is different because of Trey's work," he says. "The creation of our homeless ministry and the increasingly sustained voice of Community Interfaith are changing the political climate of the city in a new and very helpful way." A glimpse of Christ's reign, perhaps?

chapter 6

Transforming the Story

• *Carole* •

On this day after Epiphany, Carole and I can see through the window of her study that looks out into the parish hall of St. Thomas Church, where stacks of organ pipes await installation in the sanctuary and scattered Christmas decorations will soon be boxed up until Advent comes again. Her part-time assistant has gone for the day, and we sip tea as she tells me about her ministry with this pastoral-size parish.[1] Getting up from the sofa to retrieve a slim volume from her desk, she hands me the book, saying, "Maybe this will give you some perspective on the challenges of a ministry like mine." The book, *If You Meet George Herbert on the Road, Kill Him* by Justin Lewis-Anthony, decries the idealized model for parish ministry depicted in the nearly legendary stories of George Herbert's "country parson."[2] Lewis-Anthony, a priest in the Church of England, demythologizes Herbert's legacy and argues forcefully against the impossible expectations placed upon ordinary parish clergy, offering instead a more accessible vision for a fruitful and sustainable pastoral life.

Carole's ministry at St. Thomas has been, to the casual observer, a fairly ordinary one. The church has about 110 families on its rolls, with Sunday attendance hovering around one hundred, just as it was when she came twenty years ago. Some who were there at that time have died or moved on, and some new members have been born, baptized, or transferred into the parish. The church has a new roof (more about that later) and a new parking lot, and soon it will have a new pipe organ, but otherwise it looks from the outside pretty much the same as it did when she arrived. The sameness causes Don, a former pastor of another denomination who has found a congenial church home here, to wonder whether Carole has really been mostly a "caretaker" for all these years. "What would it have been like," he asks himself, "if she had projected a vision for St. Thomas?" And then, responding to his own question, he adds, "Or maybe her vision was to maintain things as they are; not to evangelize but to care effectively for this group of shepherds in the field."

Carole is, to be sure, a natural caretaker, albeit with an acquired ability to take care of herself as well. She came to ministry a long way round, growing up with a Southern Baptist mother and a Yankee Episcopalian father, and her childhood experiences helped her see that there is always more than one way to view a situation. Although she was baptized as a youth, she says, by the time she graduated from high school she had become an atheist. Some college courses in religion moved her into an agnosticism that fit with her plans to be an environmental research scientist, intent on finding ways to care for the earth. Over several years she tentatively began to explore Christian community and practice while launching her scientific career until, quite by surprise, she says, she felt a call to attend seminary. Not yet sure that she was headed for parish ministry, she immersed herself at a conservative theological school in a study of theology and the practice of ministry, which eventually led to her ordination and an initial call as associate pastor of a large church. There she thinks she was well mentored by the congregation's senior pastor.

Just as she was contemplating moving on to become a solo pastor, one of her seminary professors invited her to join the staff of a seminary where he had just become dean. Accepting the invitation, she found that her job in this very ecumenical setting was to nurture students, raise money, and direct church relations. While there, she also was drawn into an informal niche as a role model for women seminarians that was then expanded by the local bishop, who sent her on several interviews with churches looking for a new pastoral leader, getting these churches accustomed to considering a woman pastor. Through these interviews she came to understand that parishes could have personality types, just like pastors, and so she began to see how compatibility on the Myers-Briggs Type Indicator might be a vitally important factor in considering a call. One of her interviews led to an invitation to be pastor of a large and prestigious parish that offered the promise of rapid career advancement. But her discoveries about compatibility and her trust of her own intuition led her to see that this parish was not a fit for her, so she declined the call. When St. Thomas, a much smaller parish just across the street from a state university campus, called, however, she was clear that ministry with these thoughtful and creative introverts "felt right." Thus began the story of Carole and St. Thomas Church.

Embracing the story

Carole's life story had changed in several ways before she settled into her path of parish ministry. Experience with changes like these in her own life prepared her well for guiding the process that has resulted in transforming St. Thomas's story. Such revision has been the subtext of the unfolding story of God's people since Adam and Eve, and it is the essence of God's promise, "I am making all things new" (Rev. 21:5). It is people like Carole, through mundane pastoral routines with ordinary groups like St. Thomas Church, who become harbingers of the extraordinary truth of such hope.

Before stories can change, however, they must first be heard and understood. In their book *Know Your Story and Lead with It*, Richard Hester, pastoral counselor and seminary professor, and Kelli Walker-Jones, pastor and seminary field-education coordinator, describe an approach to narrative leadership based on their research carried out through their North Carolina "Sustaining Pastoral Excellence" project funded by the Lilly Endowment. Hester and Walker-Jones describe the importance of pastors' understanding and drawing upon their personal stories in leading congregations. Carole's leadership of St. Thomas church has built upon that awareness of her own life story and has blended her story with a sensitive understanding of the church's story. The result has been a parish whose life has been revitalized as their collective story has been transformed.

Carole recalls that when she came to St. Thomas, the congregation was always in crisis. Coping with crisis, in fact, seemed to be the parish's defining characteristic, and dependence upon clergy leadership to solve the crisis had become a pattern. She says, "There never seemed to be enough money, the building was falling apart, and the budget was fifty thousand dollars out of whack." But she was drawn to the people who were there, and she felt a compatibility with their predominantly cerebral expression of faith that undergirded their identity as an intellectually curious and theologically liberal congregation.

She thinks one of the questions asked at her interview was especially revealing: "What would you do if after Easter you discovered the lilies needed watering?" Her answer—"I would water them and then find out whose responsibility it was to keep them watered"—differed markedly from the previous pastor's approach. "He just watered them himself, and eventually he became exhausted because he took on everything," she says. While her predecessor's approach may have been an improvement over *his* predecessor's ("he just didn't water at all"), Carole sensed early in her ministry at St. Thomas that the path of over-responsibility would not work for her or, in the long run, for the church. Changing the story of the church from being crisis-driven and clergy-dependent was necessary for both her own and the church's well-being.

The change agent

But how? What has made it possible for Carole to help St. Thomas craft a new narrative? She has certainly employed some intentional strategies in this transformative pastoral work, and we will look specifically at those shortly. But the success of these strategies is grounded, I think, in Carole's clear understanding of her own story channeled into her fundamental approach to leadership.

Carole recalls being very clear when she came to St. Thomas that there were no easy fixes for the challenges facing the church. But she was determined to remain calm herself, and the message she conveyed was "We'll fix it together." Carole's ordination to ministry had taken place on the Feast of the Annunciation, celebrating the time when Mary calmly replied to the angel Gabriel's apparently ludicrous announcement that she would give birth to the Savior of the world, "Let it be unto me according to your word." Carole wonders whether she has incorporated some of that unflappable attitude into her own life and practice of pastoral ministry, beginning with the surprising acquiescence she felt when she first sensed a call to go to seminary.

Diane, who joined the church eight years ago when she moved to town and not long afterward became Carole's paid assistant in the parish office, notes, "Part of Carole's success is that she is centered within herself—she knows who she is, both good and bad." That fundamental integrity has allowed her to retain her own sense of self in her work, while responding with integrity to the needs of the world as she perceives them. In her faith, she appears to have lived what nineteenth-century Jesuit Jean Pierre de Caussade called "abandonment to divine providence" in his book by the same name. In her work with the parish, she has practiced what Edwin Friedman, the contemporary family-systems author and consultant, called "non-anxious presence." Whatever it may be called, however, Carole's tranquil hope seems to have inspired the parish's self-confidence.

Carole believes that the calmness of her leadership has also helped the parish withstand the waves of antagonism from the previous bishop and others in the larger church who repeatedly rebuked the St. Thomas parish, and Carole herself, for their liberal theological leanings. She thinks the assault she felt contributed to a systemic shift within the congregation that allowed members to set aside their own internal conflicts to join in facing the threat they experienced from outside. At the same time, Carole began to feel protective of the congregation against these threats. That sense of greater community in the church and her own sense of protectiveness has contributed to Carole's own shift in thinking about the longevity of her ministry, extending her original expectation that she might be at St. Thomas only seven or eight years. Ettajane, who joined the parish fifteen years ago, sees Carole's protectiveness as a sign of her strength: "She refuses to be beaten into submission," she says, "and she remains a truth speaker."

Carole's matter-of-fact honesty has also fostered a climate of trust in the congregation that is a vital product of her leadership. Ettajane thinks the basis of that trust is to be found in Carole's serene introverted personality: "Carole's spirit spreads out over the parish—a spirit of well-being, comfort, and interesting things going on." But she goes on to say that the trust is fostered in practical ways, like her ability to allow laypeople to find their own places in the church and then, using words that several others in the parish have used, being "not a micromanager." The church has learned to trust itself as a community, and the people have learned to trust one another despite their quite diverse gifts and beliefs.

Carole traces this gentle approach (which she sees as essential to her "suggestive" leadership style, described in the next section) to her mother's having "raised me to be nice." In fact, it is also a distinctively feminine approach, as linguist Deborah Tannen's research on gender communication styles demonstrates. Tannen, a Georgetown University professor and popular author, pointed out in her book *You Just Don't Understand* that women more often tend to express opinions or make suggestions in the form of questions, compared to men, who more often issue declarative statements.[3] Dave, who served on the search committee that called Carole to St. Thomas, just thinks this is part of Carole's quiet, consensus-building approach: "It's kind of subtle. I'm not sure how it happens. You hang around for a while and begin to get into the mind-set that Carole's trying to teach us about."

At the heart of Carole's composed approach is her deep spirituality. Seen most readily in her preaching and priestly roles, Carole's identity is sustained by a disciplined spirituality. She has been a dedicated participant in a spiritual-direction group for fifteen years and cherishes her participation in an ecumenical clergy peer group. More recently she has purchased a mountain home in an eclectic community populated by groups of diverse spiritual practitioners of various faiths, and she is refreshed and renewed by regular time spent there. She says these practices and connections, along with her longstanding regular visits with "Albert the analyst," keep her aware of the need for patience in ministry as the cycles of the community and the seasons of spiritual life unfold. Recalling her scientific training, she compares the church's life to the way lakes go through cycles during the year, when the bottom gets turned over or when algae wax and wane. As she "attends" to St. Thomas, she thinks of herself as a waiter, modifying Simone Weil's image of "waiting for God" to what is for Carole a more meaningful image of "waiting on God."

Carole's most powerful role for helping St. Thomas change its story, it turns out, has been her full embrace of her priestly identity. She's not just an organizational leader, although she surely is that. But in her personal spiritual depth and her public liturgical role she has helped the congregation find a new life with greater confidence and more effective living. Just as Babette's extravagant dinner, depicted in Isak Dinesen's short story "Babette's Feast" (which has been made into a powerful film), transformed a dispirited community into a lively party, Carole's ministry has brought a joyful sense of abundant hope to St. Thomas's life, conveyed most fully and dependably at the table around which the people gather each week.

BUILDING RELATIONSHIPS AND SINCERELY CARING

Frank was a passionate advocate for peace, for the poor, and in the last years of his life, for immigrants, and he built his ministry on a commitment to social action that was recognized nationally and ecumenically. Many people marveled that he was able to be such a provocative voice for social justice—some considered him just too controversial for their taste—and yet enjoy such strong support within his own congregation. Quite simply, he did his pastoral work. Premarriage counseling wasn't just instruction; it was relationship building and pastoral support. Home visits were not something for an earlier era in Frank's mind; they were necessary parts of ministry. Building personal relationships and sincerely caring for his people, Frank was able to take ethical stands that might have gotten others burned at the stake.

Elements of transformation

Out of these personal characteristics and practices, Carole has employed several concrete strategies in reshaping the church's story. The foundation of her approach has been her use of what she calls "suggestive leadership." She is aware that this approach is sometimes frustrating to the retired military colonels in her parish who are more accustomed to a command structure. (She has found, however, that on those few occasions when she does become directive, it is the colonels who sometimes are most resistant.) She knows that she actually has a broad repertoire of styles, but she usually begins with suggesting, as in, "Wouldn't it be helpful if we found people with financial gifts to take responsibility for this issue?"

Ettajane is grateful for Carole's suggestive approach, contrasting it with the style of a pastor in a previous parish who liked to get his own way. "It was part of his job to get his own way, I think. His style was 'I can make that judgment because I'm the priest.'" This "Father knows best" model of pastoral leadership has characterized the church for centuries, but Western democratic societies and especially the growing number of women clergy in Protestant churches are rapidly consigning this patriarchal style to the refuse bin of the church's history. For Carole, this suggestive approach goes hand in hand with her commitment to empowering leaders in the parish. She may be the catalyst for activity and change, but as she says, "Clergy come and go. St. Thomas is not my church; it's their church. Well, of course, it's God's church finally, but it's really our church together."

Don sees how Carole's suggestive approach corresponds to what he calls her ministry of encouragement. He was surprised, for example, by her inviting him, despite his background in another denomination, to teach a class on church membership. She has also encouraged him and other clergy who are members of the parish to preach "whenever we want." And he has seen her encourage members of the church board to take on tasks in which they are interested. Dave says Carole just "allows these things to happen," saying, "Let's run with it and see where it goes." For him, that meant feeling her encouragement in launching a Habitat for Humanity house-building project, or working on a program of outreach to children with AIDS. Pat, a longtime member, adds that Carole's approach is always "Let's work on that together," which she thinks allows people to try out their ideas with her support.

Diane thinks one of the richest examples of Carole's encouraging can be seen in the candidate for ministry who has emerged from the parish in the past several years. She remembers how Carole invited this woman to assume various leadership roles that have prepared her for this journey toward ordination. She especially recalls a delicate situation involving another parishioner who needed attention and how Carole encouraged this emerging leader to trust her own ability to respond appropriately.

Her approach—to take care of things and then to empower others to take greater responsibility—became a central strategy of Carole's leadership and a primary means of helping the people of St. Thomas reimagine their church's story in new ways. Diane has heard Carole rail occasionally at "those who always expect the pastor to take care of it." Diane is sure that Carole actually could almost always take care of it if she applied herself to the task, and she is also sure that Carole has full confidence in herself that she could. But she admires the fact that Carole is "willing to stay out of the way and let folks stumble through. Getting out of the way does give guidance in its own way."

Carole's role in helping St. Thomas craft this new narrative has been both priestly and pastoral. She has become, in Lewis-Anthony's words recalling imagery from Archbishop of Canterbury Rowan Williams, a *weaver* of confident community. In a 2004 speech on "The Christian Priest Today," Williams declared that the pastor's job is to help the church become

> a kind of space cleared by God through Jesus in which people may become what God made them to be (God's sons and daughters), and that what we have to do about the church is not first to organize it as a society but to inhabit it as a climate or a landscape. . . . It is a place or dimension in the universe that is in some way growing towards being the universe itself in restored relation to God.[4]

Carole's empowering pastoral care for the people, delivered out of her core identity as liturgical leader of the parish, has somehow allowed her to weave together an ordinary group of people into an extraordinary Christian community.

Like other aspects of her ministry, Carole's approach to liturgical leadership is inclusive. She emphasizes the importance of this shared work by saying, "Lots of people take responsibility for parts [of the liturgy]. I make sure the structures are in place, but it's truly the work of the people." But through her leadership, Carole has also become the "parson" of the parish, the incarnational manifestation of the corporate body and the spiritual and liturgical heart of the parish. Her intellectual and theological views inform and persuade primarily through her preaching, while undergirding the vital prayer and liturgy so central to the parish. Dave notes that when Carole was named canon liturgist of the diocese, it was a very good fit because her love for and practice of liturgy are so central to who she is and how she practices ministry.

One unique strategy Carole employed to help the church revise its story was her "Murder Mysteries and Theology" book discussion group. Maybe the group was begun just for fun, a stimulating community-building activity for a group of bookish Christians. But several of those I talked with about Carole's ministry cited this group as particularly significant in the life of the parish. As the group read and discussed theological themes and ethical dilemmas in a series of murder mysteries, Ettajane recalls that a central question consistently emerged: "Is this person redeemable?" Ettajane, and no doubt others in the group, learned convincingly that "Carole thinks everybody is redeemable." It may well be that the real-life "mystery of the crisis-driven and leader-dependent church" was resolved by Carole as she herself became the brilliant detective who solved the mystery and proclaimed redemption for the church.

Changes in St. Thomas's story are not mere sociological shifts in a social community. At the heart of the church's transformation is a genuine *metanoia*. This changed perception in the congregation is most visibly enacted and upheld in corporate worship, which all at St. Thomas agree is their foundation. Dave says, "Being at communion every Sunday is our core. . . . Our service to the community derives from worship. Worship is *fundamental* to our church, and attendance is high."

Diane sees how Carole's leadership has made this connection so clearly: "Liturgy is the heart of her leadership. She has a deep, deep understanding and love of being a priest. Carole not only connects to God through the liturgy, but she helps the rest of us connect as well. She has the ability to bring Scripture down to earth and put it in front of us as everyday life." Listening to the people of St. Thomas convinces an observer that when the congregation gathers, the worshipers sense, through Carole's leadership, that the holy truly dwells among them. Worship has become a genuine avenue for the manifestation of the divine in their common life together. As a result of this lively worship, when Carole-the-liturgical-leader makes a pastoral call or leads a book discussion group, the connection to God is readily made. But it is not, as Ettajane says, the force of Carole's personality that carries this reality—quite the opposite. Once again, it is her calmness, patience, and collaborative spirit that convey God's presence.

A new story

It is this collaborative spirit emerging throughout Carole's ministry that has transformed St. Thomas's story into a new narrative. "It is my responsibility to lead people into greater responsibility for the parish," she insists, and one can see the results of her efforts in the church today. Dave has seen this commitment in Carole emerge and grow over the years. "It's a work in progress for twenty years," he says, noting that she has become adept at getting others to take responsibility. "The parish has become much more cohesive," he observes, "more willing to do things for itself and not wait for ecclesiastical authority." He continues to admire and appreciate her gentle but firm efforts at delegating, even though he sees that "she struggles with that—she wants to do it all but knows it's not good for either her or the church."

Carole's empowering approach has led, it seems, to a congregation that has learned to believe in its own resourcefulness. The pastor no longer has to water the lilies, at least most of the time, because lay leaders now usually step up to the tasks at hand. St. Thomas's story has gone from one largely characterized by dependence on the ministrations of an ecclesiastical leader to becoming *ecclesia*—those who are called out to be God's people.

The congregation's growing sense of self-confidence began to develop during the early years of Carole's ministry at St. Thomas, and it blossomed most visibly when the church faced an economic crisis while she was on sabbatical about eight years into her ministry. A leaky roof during the heavy rains led to terrible damage to the wooden floors of the sanctuary, and although insurance covered the cost of repairing the floor, the expensive roof repair was a cost that the church would have to bear itself. Carole was preparing to go overseas when she received the call from lay leaders telling her of the problem, and she questioned whether she should go in the midst of this crisis. But the leaders assured her they could handle it, and they did. Money was raised to cover the unbudgeted major expenses, and laypeople energetically pitched in and took on jobs like painting that they could handle. After Carole returned, the church built upon the crisis, not only by developing a careful facilities plan for the future but also by expanding members' notions of stewardship, a step that has fostered higher giving not only to the church's needs but also to mission and outreach ministries.

"Calamity was the motivator," Pat recalls, "and it provided the stimulus for the congregation to work together and raise the money and do the work ourselves. Carole was very much in the background of all that. The people did it." When Carole returned from her sabbatical and found the progress that the church had made in addressing the problems, she was understandably quite pleased. But she thinks the people themselves were even more pleased. As Carole puts it, "They were proud to have showed Mom they could handle things on their own."

The circumstances surrounding the church's recovery from the leaky roof became, Carole believes, the foundation for the church's new narrative. While some of the characteristics of St. Thomas remained constant—its academic liberal faith, its comfort with its modest size, its restrained but genuine hospitality, its grounding in liturgical life—some new self-understandings have taken shape. Now the church sees itself as stable, not only financially but also in its self-confidence as a parish. In developmental categories, it has gone from being the naughty and not very competent child ("We were the bad kid on the block," Diane says) to becoming the mature adult. In psychological terms, the church has gained ego strength. In biblical language, the group that was once "few in number and of little account" (Ps. 105:12), as the psalmist once described the people of Israel, has become a people who know their worth and who can claim their identity as God's "anointed ones."

This tender new narrative must now, of course, survive the challenges of a harsh economy, continuing denominational strife, and the prospect of Carole's departure from the scene in the next few years. Anxiety about a leadership transition has already begun to emerge, prompted by the invitation a year or so ago for Carole to become a candidate for bishop in another diocese. Although she eventually declined the invitation, she and the congregation both were reminded that her time as pastor of St. Thomas would come to an end before very long. As Pat says, "It makes me nervous when she starts to talk about retiring."

Beyond the core principles of self-confidence and hope, what will endure in this new revised standard version of St. Thomas's story? Carole has already begun to think carefully about this question as she considers her own transition into a new phase of her life. She has helped the congregation launch a "dream-catchers" group as a forum within which the church might do some planning for the future. Not surprisingly, however, she expresses confidence that St. Thomas will continue to live out its own call as a church in as-yet-uncharted ways, enabled by a strengthened leadership corps, with solid grounding in prayer and worship and, most of all, a trust in the members themselves as a people of God. She sees that whatever endures after she is gone will be the result of God's "regard for this vine," as the psalmist expresses it (Ps. 80:14).

Ettajane thinks that the physical improvements in the church and some of the programs will continue to be significant after Carole leaves. She also says that Carole's identity as a female leader has been so satisfying that she can't imagine having a male pastor again. Dave agrees that Carole's ministry will have an enduring impact, noting that outreach efforts such as the congregation's involvement in Habitat for Humanity will be a lasting result of Carole's leadership. He goes on to express his confidence in the enduring effects of the spiritual deepening that he himself has found and that he believes the congregation as a whole has experienced. "She has been a significant spiritual mentor to all of us," he says.

Don also thinks this spiritual energizing will last. "I see a vibrancy about the church," he says, and he is grateful for the various ways she has been his pastor and wise counselor, helping him sort things out at times and also caring for him when he was hospitalized ten years ago. Carole's personal ministrations have been important to many in the parish, including Pat, who especially appreciates Carole's guidance in "learning how to deal with things I can't control. My faith is stronger—in fact, she really helped me find it, because I don't come from a strong religious background." Carole's suggestive leadership and ministry of encouragement, practiced at the congregational level, have clearly also been a part of her pastoral-care ministry as well.

Diane believes what is most important in the parish will certainly survive—that is, its spirit of hospitality toward all sorts of people based in a profound understanding of the high calling for the church to be a genuine community of the Divine on earth. "Carole has been very purposeful about engendering in this group the idea that our job on this earth is to truly love one another. There is such a strong sense of that here that I don't think anyone could destroy it."

Most fundamentally, the story of St. Thomas, including the ways it has been transformed during the years of Carole's pastoral leadership into a church of confident abundance, will survive. The themes and anecdotes of the story are already being recited again and again, as I have heard from various members in the course of my queries about Carole. And the story will continue to unfold, of course, while Carole is still here and after she has gone. It must, after all, be told and retold again, identifying and interpreting God's continuing activity in the church's life and ministry. That's been the way of God's people from the beginning. The people of St. Thomas—Dave and Pat and Don and Diane and Ettajane and many others—will continue to be both actors and storytellers in the ongoing drama, and others will come in the future to join the cast. While Carole may seem to be playing the lead these days, her role will eventually come to be seen as simply a major supporting actor. As Dave says, "She was never interested in being 'the great leader.' That's not her style." Carole has found that more realistic pastoral life, and it has fostered a fruitful story.

chapter 7

Connecting with Spirit

• *Sue* •

S ue lives out her ministry walking the narrow path between charism and institution," observed Fran, as we
talked one bright autumn morning at Santa Maria de
la Vid, the Norbertine priory where he lives mostly as a
hermit among his brother monks. He's describing Sue's
creative ministry, one foot firmly set in the institutional church
and the other on the unique path of a spiritual renewal program
she leads for pastors and parishes. Fran knows both Sue and this
holy terrain of service very well because he has devoted most of
his own fifty years of ministry to the care and healing of clergy. In
three of those years he has partnered with Sue in developing and
leading spiritual renewal retreats for small ecumenical groups of
pastors from throughout the country. "Sue's pastoral leadership
transcends the institution," he continues. "It's like when we were
a catacomb community, when we didn't think the Gentiles could
be part of the community until the deepness of connection became
inescapable. This work she's doing goes under the walls of division
to a deeper unity, a deeper connection."

Fran is one of the reasons Sue is leading this ministry of retreats
and workshops. He was on the steering committee that interviewed
her for the job, and when she returned home from the interview,
she told her husband, "This is a holy man, and the opportunity to

work with him feels like an incredible gift." But it's the ministry, not the man, to which Sue feels called. The call is deep, and it goes back a long way.

Sue experienced her call to ordained ministry at a church camp in high school. She wasn't sure she was being called to be a parish pastor, but she knew she was called to ministry of some kind instead of to her childhood dream of becoming a prosecuting attorney. "It never felt like a decision to go into ministry," she says, "but it was a claim that had been staked on me somehow." She remembers with great appreciation her relationship with Sharon, the church youth director during her high-school years, and she thought initially that youth ministry might be her own focus, because she believed at the time that "that's what women do." So she went to a church-related college and began to work in a program aimed at helping young people consider church vocations. She continued that work through her college years and then went on to seminary, supporting herself as a youth director and later as manager of a religious bookstore. While she was completing her master of divinity degree, however, she grew more skeptical about becoming ordained. She didn't like the way her church treated women, and she was troubled by her church's official stance on social-justice issues, especially its refusal to ordain openly gay and lesbian people.

During her college and seminary days, Sue had been drawn to spiritual retreats and active spiritual disciplines. She went to the Shalem Institute in Washington, D.C., to receive training in spiritual direction and came back to her college and seminary campuses to lead students in prayer groups. She attended training events sponsored by the United Methodist–related Upper Room in Nashville and was energized by the ideas and practices she learned there. As her own prayer life deepened, she began to see that deepening the spiritual lives of pastors and laypeople could be central to her ministry.

Sue married Bert while she was in seminary, and when he was invited to take a campus-ministry position on the West Coast, she happily followed him there. In their new judicatory she found a more tolerant and even progressive spirit than she had known in her previous settings, so she put aside her resistance to "final vows" and gave herself over to becoming an ordained minister in good standing. Her first parish was a small rural church where the mostly older members warmly welcomed their new young preacher. They appreciated her hopeful energy, her good preaching, her humble demeanor and lively humor, and especially her sincere concern for their personal lives. As she moved into this pastoral ministry, she found "her own deep gladness and the world's deep need" coming together, just as Fredrick Buechner had described the ideal vocation.[1]

Sue was quite surprised, though, by the reticence she found among the members when she inquired about their spiritual lives. "They looked at the floor when I asked about prayer, and I was incredulous. I said, 'You mean no one has ever asked you about your prayer life before?'" So she began to lead prayer groups and teach classes on spiritual disciplines. She formed small groups where these longtime Christians began, many for the first time, to tell their personal stories of growth in faith. "Talking with seventy- and eighty-year-old people about their spiritual journeys was amazing," she recalls, and her own heart quickened as she listened to these touching stories. As people in the groups shared their experiences with one another and began to pray together more earnestly, she found the life of the congregation becoming richer and Sunday worship becoming more lively.

Sue's work with spiritual renewal began to be noticed throughout her judicatory, and she soon found herself appointed head of the committee charged with nurturing clergy development. She began forming clergy prayer groups and organizing retreats throughout the region, and connections between pastors were strengthened as spiritual lives deepened. At about the same time, her husband's large urban church, next to the campus where he had formerly been campus minister, began experimenting with a contemporary worship service on Sunday evenings, but the congregation was having trouble finding the right leadership. Soon a bartering arrangement was struck that allowed Sue to come to the urban church to lead these Sunday evening services in exchange for support the urban church provided to Sue's rural congregation.

It was not long, though, before Sue moved from the rural church where she had served for six years to a post as associate pastor of evangelism in a team ministry with her husband at the urban church. And so it was that Sue found herself serving the dream congregation she had literally envisioned in a Quaker "clearness" meeting a number of years earlier. Here was a progressive and faithful congregation of believers who were both intellectually curious and positively inclined to explore contemplative prayer and practice. She was in her own pastoral heaven—until she saw a job ad in *The Christian Century* magazine.

> Director for new program in clergy spirituality. Ordained with at least seven years parish experience. Must understand counseling and spiritual disciplines. Ecumenical and judicatory experience valuable. Excellent organizational, speaking, and writing skills required.

The ad caught her eye two days before Christmas, and she couldn't sleep that night, thinking of all the things she had done so far in her ministry that fit the bill. "What if everything you've done so far in life is to prepare you for this?" she asked herself. Because she had never before written a resume, she had to buy a book on how to write one. Her resume cataloguing her skills and experience got her an interview, and her vision for the possibilities in this new ministry, combined with her authenticity and passion, got her the job.

For the past seven years, Sue has been leader of an ecumenical program that "aims to foster sustained excellence in ministry by cultivating in participating clergy vital prayer and spiritual practice integrated with the resources of psychology and community. The program invites clergy and the systems within which they live and work into a process of formation and re-formation for sustaining pastoral excellence." With principal funding from the Lilly Endowment, this program is one of sixty-three programs throughout the country that Lilly has supported through its "Sustaining Pastoral Excellence" initiative. Through this effort, Sue and her coworkers have touched the lives of several hundred pastors from across the country in a series of retreats and prayer/support groups based in communities across the southwestern United States. Now moving into the second phase of the project, the program is broadening its emphasis to cultivate deeper spiritual vitality in congregations as well as serving the clergy themselves. Some of the participants are ministers who participated in the early retreats, accompanied by teams of leaders from their congregations, while others are teams of clergy and lay leaders from parishes who are new to the process.

Leaving the parish to go into this more programmatic ministry was hard for Sue, and she misses the work of a congregational minister. "My heart never left the parish," Sue says as she describes her current ministry. "I still miss it—a lot. The rhythm, sharing people's journeys, preaching, crafting worship—these are all precious activities. I have never felt relief at being out of the parish." She remains deeply engaged in the life of the parish she attends regularly, and she recently contracted with that parish to provide some leadership when the pastor goes on sabbatical for a few months.

She thinks the biggest difference between her current ministry and the parishes where she once served is the rhythm of her life. While she still accepts every invitation she can to be a guest preacher in various churches, the weekly cycle of preparing sermons and planning worship for a familiar congregation is missing, replaced by preparation for the intensity of four-day contemplative retreats, concentrated teaching/learning workshops, and small groups of pastors who meet weekly for prayer and sharing. The connections are very different as well, shifting from the comfortable pastoral relationship with people in their ordinary lives to a more intense connection with retreatants and workshop participants over a set-apart span of days. As a strong extrovert, Sue notes that she has gone "from an extrovert's dream job in a lively and progressive parish to an introvert's dream job leading frequent contemplative experiences and spending long hours at my desk planning and writing."

This unique vocation is clearly ministry in Sue's mind and in the eyes of others who work with her in various ways. She has always been disturbed that denominations frequently do not clearly recognize nonparochial ministries as "real ministry." Now that she sees how desperately pastors and lay leaders need this spiritual deepening offered through this ministry, she is even more enthusiastic about the significance of her work. "I'm often walking on holy ground," she says, and she is both excited and humbled by the opportunity she has to lead this specialized ministry to clergy and congregations.

Connecting with people

Sue believes that despite the differences in rhythms, the skills and leadership required in her current ministry are not so different from those required in the parish, beginning with the ability to connect with people and help them understand what you have to offer. She compares the first meeting with a group of pastors on retreat or lay leaders in a workshop to walking into a cold hospital room for a pastoral visit. Both encounters require warm and careful listening to the circumstances and needs of people, along with creating space for the people to hear God's voice. Both situations require the pastor to let go of her need to have the right answers, so that people can find their own way forward with God's help. And both require clarity in the minister's own mind about the mission to which she is called. The pastoral task in both these settings remains constant.

Catherine, a minister who has been in one of Sue's prayer and support groups for three years, recalls with great appreciation Sue's pastoral skills at the beginning of their relationship. Catherine had been serving as pastor of her parish for only a few months when her son had to undergo serious surgery. "Sue just seemed to know what the depths were, knew what the pit was like—not living in it like I was, but acquainted with it. She was able to be with me going through that surgery in a deep and very supportive way." When she heard that Sue was launching a group for women clergy, Catherine was immediately drawn to the idea. She liked the ecumenical dimension, but she felt especially drawn to the possibility of deepening relationships with other women. Her best friend had died fairly recently of ovarian cancer, and she was still grieving that loss. "I just trusted Sue," Catherine says, and since others spoke so highly of Sue's leadership skills, she quickly agreed to join the group.

"What I appreciate about Sue," Catherine goes on to say, "is that she's the leader, but she's also part of the group. She is able to be vulnerable with us, but she can also accept that there's not always time for her. She's been very open with us, and that's been a wonderful lesson for me in managing my own dual roles. Part of the power of her leadership is her willingness to be fully who she is."

For Catherine, Sue's openness has offered a new model for her own pastoral work. "I was formed in a way that says: if you are the pastor, you don't become friends with folks. You don't let anyone see your dirty laundry. I always thought that was kind of stupid." Catherine sees clearly the importance of keeping clear boundaries with people in the church, and she understands quite well the destructive consequences when pastors have sometimes crossed boundaries inappropriately. But until she formed a relationship with Sue as a pastoral leader, she had no good models for how a pastor might share her real self while still retaining her pastoral identity. Catherine believes Sue's example is an approach especially suited for women, and she is now experimenting with this "feminine" way of leadership that permits vulnerability and even friendship with parishioners while remaining in the pastoral role. "As I have moved from being mostly a stay-at-home mom and switched roles with my husband to become a full-time installed pastor, Sue's modeling and encouragement have been very important to me." Now, as her staff grows, Catherine is applying these lessons to a new dimension as a female head of staff "in a feminine mom kind of way."

Bert, Sue's now former husband, with whom she was copastor, continues to admire her relational style of leadership. He recalls how quickly she connected with those who were attending the evening service at their shared parish. "She spoke the language of Generation X, and lots of students showed up and stayed active. Even her preaching was connectional, biblical in approach, and contemporary in its application." He also remembers how she fostered connections among the disparate group of musicians who provided contemporary music in that service, allowing them to put it together themselves. Sue's relational style, Bert says, was a perfect fit for her job as minister of evangelism, in which she gave leadership to a witnessing style of outreach for the congregation. "She's a good listener," he adds, "and responds to people with integrity that builds genuine community. But she's also able to teach people how to share their faith in their own words."

Fran believes Sue's capacity to connect with other people and encourage them to be more relational makes her an excellent pastor to pastors—"a vicar for priests," as he refers to her role, drawing on his Roman Catholic tradition. Over the years, he has seen her put together a kind of "ministry to ministers anonymous," which allows pastors in her retreats and groups to share deeply about their own journeys with confidence that their privacy will be honored. He attributes that capacity in large part to the non-institutional nature of her work, lived out in ecumenical groups without fear of judgment or control by some church hierarchy. Fran is sure this approach cultivates a climate of safety and depth that cuts through barriers and brings about what be believes is a "mystical ecumenism, a spiritual connection of hearts."

Sue is definitely a community builder, and her people skills are some of her greatest gifts in ministry. She herself recognizes, however, that she still has much to learn about the practical mechanics of delivering ministry within organizational structures. Bert notes that she is much more gifted relationally than administratively and remembers that she sometimes had difficulty understanding the competing budgetary demands in a larger church. Sue acknowledges that working with budgets is not her strength, although her current program leadership position within a larger nonprofit organization has given her opportunity and training to help her become more adept in financial management. It's no surprise that her growth in this area comes especially through her relational abilities, which she brings to negotiations with her supervisor and the organization's business manager as well as with her peers on the staff.

Her pastoral skills of listening, spiritual vitality, attentiveness to the needs of individuals, awareness of group dynamics, ability to think theologically—all these equip Sue well for the informal role she has begun to carry in the interfaith ministry where she now works. Her colleagues easily think of her as a pastor or a chaplain, and she is often called upon to lead prayer or perform pastoral functions in the group. While she certainly must manage her program, she is "more model than manager," as Fran puts it, living out her pastoral identity as a program leader together with a diverse group of colleagues who perform some quite different kinds of work.

Sue understands that her capacity to foster community is a central part of her ministry. Whether in an ecumenical group of clergy on retreat, a prayer group of elderly farmers in a parish, a diverse collection of church musicians, or an eclectic team of program leaders, Sue creates small communities that might be examples of the "circles of trust" that Parker Palmer, one of Sue's mentors, describes in his book *A Hidden Wholeness*. The necessary heart of such community, Palmer suggests, is recognition of the tough but shy soul of each participant in the group that "like a wild animal, hides in the underbrush waiting for opportunity to appear. . . . The last thing we should do is go crashing through the woods yelling for it to come out," Palmer advises. "But if we will walk quietly into the woods, sit patiently at the base of a tree, breathe with the earth, and fade into our surroundings, the wild creature we seek might put in an appearance."[2]

Incorporating Palmer's ideas into her work with groups is one of the primary ways Sue understands and provides for the expression of spirituality. The principal resource she employs in this approach is an embrace of silence. This may sound strange for an extrovert like Sue, but she explains that *silence in community* is the vital key to genuine community. While she respects the solitary spirituality of introverts and the life of hermits such as Fran, she believes it is in the connection to and through community that one's spirituality deepens and comes to flower. Bringing this understanding to her work as a leader, she believes that leadership should be nurtured in silence but practiced in community. It is never a solo activity. "Just as preaching is engagement with people in the pews and therefore an exercise in community," she says, "leadership requires listening together and dreaming together." For Sue, community is the necessary counterpoint to the *via negativa*, the individual's path of mystical spirituality, and silence together with others, she believes, is the vital ingredient that fosters richness in both community and ministry.

Connecting with God

This emphasis on the importance of community to a growing spiritual life demonstrates Sue's deeply incarnational theology, which undergirds her pastoral leadership and her passion for her current ministry. While she embraces a certain inner mysticism in her own spiritual practice, her life work demonstrates her belief that it is through God's presence among us as a person and through God's gathering of communities of worship and friendship and service that one encounters the divine most fully. Yet she also recognizes that these human connections can draw us away from the holy, so she strives to maintain the balance between the worldly and the divine in her own life, and to foster this balance in the lives of ministers with whom she works.

Sue is convinced that spiritual vitality is the heart of sustained excellence in ministry. Although most clergy enter ordained ministry as a genuine vocation, and for nearly all of them that vocation emerges from a vital spiritual encounter, she has found that the practice of ministry too often leads her fellow pastors into arid lands of discouragement and despair. Such disconnection from God, she has seen, too often leads clergy to become barren and dry. "The practical demands of parish life can consume the pastor's time and draw him or her away from Sabbath rest and intimacy with the holy," she says, adding, "Congregational routine and conflict can overwhelm pastors with the mundane and even the distasteful aspects of God's people. A sense of divine abandonment can flow from this experience, fostering a diminution of energies and diversion of values, leading seasoned and skilled ministers away from ministry."

Sue's focus of ministry grows out of her concern that the church has neglected the spiritual lives of its ministers. She has often heard from clergy that once they have had their sense of call assessed by psychologists and boards and bishops, they are sent forth to study and serve with an emphasis on the church's need for them to be productive and ethical, but with little attention to their personal need for continuing spiritual nurture. Fran shares Sue's conviction that "ministry can lose its soul when it becomes preoccupied with the business of church and the demands of the institution." In their work together, Sue and Fran have frequently heard pastors confess that they do not often engage in personal prayer, and what's more, no one asks them about their prayer life. These ministers speak longingly about going on retreat, but their congregations won't give them time off, or expect them to be on call for pastoral emergencies during the retreat, or force them to choose between retreat and family vacation. Sue and Fran have also found that when ministers go through the inevitable deserts of life, they are ashamed to admit it or to seek guidance, sadly believing that they are alone, that their emotional pain is somehow their fault, and that it will impede their careers.

Because of these experiences and beliefs, Sue is determined to prod and lead the church in making spiritual-growth opportunities more widely available and generously supported. She is seeking to build habits and structures that foster spiritual growth systematically within congregations and judicatories as well as among more informal networks of clergy. She begins her commitment to this work with her own practice. Bert says that Sue is "a searching person on a quest for wholeness of life expressed in connection with God." This hunger leads her, he says, to become deeply immersed in the world precisely because of her spiritual yearnings and her desire for satisfying relationships. Fran also sees this spiritual core in Sue's ministry, calling it "Spirit-led." He believes that she models this ministry through her own spiritual deepening and her way of networking spiritually with others, something he calls "a spiritual connection of hearts." She has, he says, "a great spiritual thirst and wants her own self to be transformed even as she assists the transformation of others."

Catherine sees Sue's spiritual authenticity particularly in the way she leads groups.

> When she asks each group member, after a time of silence, "How is it with your soul?" I think she's genuinely interested in our answers as a way of joining with each of us. And even though that way of asking is not part of my tradition, it has come to feel comfortable somehow. Now the question has evolved to "When have you seen God's grace in your life?" and the process of sharing continues to take new forms in the group. But Sue's the one who makes it possible. She always has a candle and a cloth and always brings chocolate. It's always worship, and for many women, chocolate is sacramental!

As Catherine describes these gatherings, I can imagine these women talking and laughing around a table on which is placed a cloth and candle and chocolate, joined by the bread of their common labor in ministry and by their shared hearts, with Sue as their graceful celebrant.

Catherine is especially grateful for Sue's simple and sometimes quite vulnerable humanity in her leadership. "There's no question that Sue is a wounded healer," Catherine goes on to say, "and she speaks out of her own woundedness quite specifically. But this business of isolation is a huge problem for pastors, and so is the tendency to intellectualize everything we do. Sue's ministry calls ministers out of their isolation and out of our heads back into contact with God. As Diana Butler Bass has said so well, being brilliant is not enough." Catherine sees Sue's very human leadership infused with her vital spirituality as precisely the antidote to Protestantism's overly intellectualized tradition of preaching. "Sue is surely very bright," Catherine goes on to say, "but preaching in her life is from her whole person. She does what someone once said: Preach always; use words when necessary."

Catherine and Fran both affirm that Sue's spirituality is not just otherworldly. Her feet are firmly planted on this world's ground. "She has a wonderful sense of humor," Catherine adds, "and I can hear God laughing with us and at us and at her. I wasn't interested in spirituality that wasn't earthy, and that's what Sue brings." And that's how she practices her own personal spiritual disciplines as well.

Sue "brings the day in," as she puts it, with an hour walking outside with her Labradoodle, Sophie, and praying. These morning encounters with creation, followed by some time writing haiku or sitting at her home altar with a candle burning, connect her with God's continuing activity in the world. She says that she has long sought to "live attentively" throughout each day, noticing the events and feelings that unfold. And then, at the end of the day, she engages in an *examen*, asking herself:

Where did I see God today? Where did I give or receive love? What do I need to let go of? What am I grateful for? I used to ask these questions as I lay in bed at night, but I kept falling asleep. So for the last several years I have been writing my thoughts down before bed. I'm not good at centering prayer or even *lectio divina*. My practice has to relate to the world somehow, and when possible, be connected to other people.

The bookends of Sue's day help reinforce her commitment to being grounded spiritually even as she enters and leaves behind the mundane demands of work and life.

Accountability is a key component of her spiritual practice. For many years Sue has had one or another spiritual director with whom she talked formally at least once a month. For the past year or so, she has been without a director because Oleta, the person she was once seeing, has now become a colleague in her work, and the relationship began to feel more blurred for her. But she still cherishes her friendship with Oleta as well as with Fran, and counts them as spiritual companions with whom she discusses the challenges of life and to whom she feels accountability. From time to time she also calls one of two friends who live out of town to share spiritual journeys and seek advice. These relationships, along with her colleagues at work and her connection to church, are part of her own spiritual community, and being part of this community is a central component of her lifetime commitment to being accountable to her call from God.

Now that she is not serving a parish, the rhythms of her spiritual life and practice have changed, just as her ministry has changed. In the parish she used the Upper Room's *Companions in Christ* curriculum with groups, and this gave her and them an opportunity to try out a variety of spiritual practices. In the parish her spiritual life was often shaped by the seasons of the church year. She explains:

> The seasons were good for me because my attention span is so short, and I do struggle with consistency. But now, having a key to the Norbertine Center and doing a lot of my work in that sacred place causes my spiritual life to be more landscape-oriented, centered in a place. I've always had an altar in my home, but now I have the benefit of that beautiful setting as a place of prayer and worship.

She sees that her spiritual life is more solitary now that she is no longer serving a parish. The year of her divorce was one of great lamentation, accentuated by her sense of aloneness. That year brought "times of intense agonies, which were followed by a kind of numbness afterward. But I think I'm recovering from all that now and feel ready to see what new chapters of spiritual growth and practice may emerge. It will be interesting to see what God has in store for me."

The principal and most tangible fruit of Sue's spiritual life remains her ministry, and she continues to fold her spiritual practice into her daily life of work.

> I do consciously attempt to have my work be a spiritual practice. I come in early when it is quiet and light a candle at my desk. I prayerfully go through my day and the people I will meet that day. I make a pot of tea and steep my morning in this practice. When I am doing something that is more soulful, like designing a new retreat, I go to the Norbertine Center,

and I am able to focus and find myself more open when the Spirit shows up. I have learned that creating space for my work, for the people who come to our programs, expands that sense of spiritual landscape I am increasingly seeing in my life.

So the routines of her day reinforce the ministry to which she is called and the values she seeks to convey to others. It's not that she's trying to be a saint, but only that she realizes she must "stay in shape" as a spiritual leader in order to live out her call.

I'VE CULTIVATED THESE TOOLS

"My first career was being an actuary for eleven years, and continuing education is an absolute necessity to doing that job well," Pat says. "So when my spiritual awakening took me to seminary, I carried that commitment to lifelong learning into my new identity on the other side of the rail. As a leader in the church, spiritual vitality is what I'm called to bring, whatever else I do and wherever I serve. When I put the collar on, that's who I am." In the face of family health issues and the challenges of parish ministry at St. Paul Church, Pat continues to practice the journaling and the centering prayer she came to know in college. "I've cultivated those tools and practiced regularly, so that I can go to that deeper center quickly whenever I find myself showing signs of becoming frayed. And that rebalances and sustains me."

Connecting with call

As Bert thinks about the surprising and sometimes painful paths that he and Sue have traveled since the years they were married and shared pastoral ministry together, he recalls a catechetical question that he and Sue discussed often: How do we know God is with us? The answer, they agreed, was this: We know that God is with us because we are being led into a place we did not intend to go. It's not that every place we end up is by God's design. But the history of God's people shows that God constantly pulls us out of our comfort and into new lands of promise. "I don't think I could have connected with anyone more deeply," Bert says, "and while I am still adjusting to the fact that we have gone our separate ways, the idea that we might not be in relationship is beyond me." Sue and Bert remain respectful friends, and both seem genuinely grateful for the time they shared together and the continuing presence of each other in their lives. Most of all, Bert is convinced that Sue's deep integrity and her sense of call to this current ministry have led her to being exactly where God wants her to be.

Fran sees Sue's decision to leave the comfort of a satisfying parish and even the security of her marriage to Bert as a sign of her fierce commitment to call that continues to characterize her ministry with ministers. "When she saw that ad in *The Christian Century,* it set her on fire, and she's still aflame with the passion of her ministry," he says. "It wasn't easy to leave the familiarity of her post as an established pastor and move across the country into a wilderness to a very different kind of work. But she is submissive to the power of the Spirit. As Gandhi imagined, she is being the change she wants to see."

As she is coming to understand her ongoing process of formation as a minister, Sue cites with appreciation the observation of Warren Bennis:

> So the point is not to become a leader. The point is to become yourself, to use yourself completely—all your skills, your gifts, your energies—in order to make your vision manifest. You must withhold nothing. You must, in sum, become the person you started out to be, and to enjoy the process of becoming.[3]

Sue is enjoying the process of becoming a spiritual leader—which is quite an audacious task to accept when you think about it. But isn't every ministry, after all, audacious? Who would dare presume to preach God's word or to direct someone on his or her journey to God or to organize God's people for pilgrimage or service? Yet that is exactly what all ministers are called to do.

The ministers who have participated in the retreats she has led and the participants in workshops and prayer/support groups she has organized are uniform in their praise of Sue's authentic leadership and their appreciation for the impact these events have had upon their lives and ministries. Dry bones are being raised to life, and spirits are being refreshed. Congregations are reclaiming their spiritual vitality. Clergy like Catherine are finding new, more feminine ideals for ministry. The models for ministry Sue has developed are being translated into different settings, like that of her colleague Patrick, a physician, who plans to offer similar retreats to physicians who suffer, like their clergy brothers and sisters, from the stress and discouragement of their work. The opportunity to reconnect with Spirit in community with others is received with gladness by all kinds of people. Sabrina, a Jewish woman who works as a children's therapist in the interfaith ministry where Sue's program is housed, said after Sue led a half-day retreat for the staff, "I am so blessed by the experience of working with good colleagues who share a connection to and appreciation for the spiritual dimension of our work."

While the fruits of her work are becoming increasingly evident, Sue is not entirely clear what the next chapters of her ministry with ministers may look like, nor does she know how her own life as a spiritual leader and a woman of God may unfold. She remains the modest and attentive person of faith she strives to be, content not to know many things. Even so, she trusts God and tries to take seriously the advice of another of her mentors, Graham Standish: "When we are humble leaders, we grow increasingly comfortable with the uncertainty that comes with trying our best to be available to God and God's guidance."[4] The taproot of Sue's pastoral leadership is being first a follower of God.

chapter 8

Bestowing Blessing

• *Paul* •

The capacity of ministers to bless people's lives has amazed me ever since I was the recipient of such blessing in my own life. When I was eleven years old and my father in his mental illness had left our home for the final time, I was invited by the pastor of our church to go fishing on a Saturday. The church had become for me an important place of stability in those uncertain days of my life—a dependable extended family. Ralph and Beulah, the pastor and his wife, invited me to spend the night at their home so we could get an early start the next day. I still recall going out with Ralph into their backyard under a brilliant starry sky, brandishing our flashlights so that we could gather some night crawlers for bait. Ralph's gift to that wounded eleven-year-old boy was a simple act of kindness involving a nighttime search for worms and a quiet morning trolling for perch on an Indiana lake. I don't remember much about the fishing, but I do remember the gift of Ralph's presence and quiet care for me in that most difficult time of my life. That church's pastor understood the power he had to make a profound difference in a young life. I felt truly blessed by his interest in sharing time with a suddenly fatherless boy, and I carry that childhood experience of blessing into my life as an adult and as a minister who tries to follow in Ralph's footsteps of teaching folks to fish.

Myron Madden, a wise hospital chaplain in New Orleans, wrote a wonderful little book years ago about the crucial importance of blessing in people's lives.[1] His insightful thesis was that many of us go through life searching, like Cain or Esau, for the blessing we did not receive from our fathers or our mothers. Maybe we were tricked out of it. Perhaps our parents did not know how to extend a blessing. Or maybe we were simply incapable of recognizing and receiving it when it was offered. But whatever the reason, Madden's observation about the human condition rings true. Many of us have not received blessing in our lives, and so we may become anxious or embittered, fearful or self-doubting, constantly searching for that unnamed mystery that we lack.

The importance of blessing and that childhood experience with my own pastor bubbled up in my mind as I began to learn more about Paul. Pastor of First Church for eighteen years, Paul is widely recognized as a "successful" minister (although he would be quick to question the meaning of that label, insisting that for him, success is staying engaged with whatever task must be addressed in the present moment). The downtown congregation he serves is large and counts a number of the community's leaders among its members, but Paul belies the stereotype of the "big steeple" preacher in many ways. He doesn't always preach on the "high holy days." He often dresses in slacks and an open-necked shirt. His enthusiastic storytelling can sometimes be a little irreverent and almost always brings a laugh or two. Although he is clearly the leader of his forty-member staff of clergy and laity, his relationships with them are relaxed and egalitarian. His wife, Nona, is not particularly active in the congregation (though she provides a vital sanctuary that helps preserve the healthiness of Paul's ministry). He sneaks off to smoke a cigarette from time to time. His comfortable home is dominated not by religious symbols, but by bulletin boards filled with photos of family and friends, and two walls displaying what he playfully calls his "shrine" to liberal political causes and campaign buttons.

Paul's career in ministry has followed a fairly traditional path. After ten years as an associate pastor in a large city, he moved to become senior pastor in a smaller community where again he stayed ten years before accepting the call to First Church. But he's aware that his personality, his approach to ministry, and especially his exercise of authority is unique. The morning of our first conversation about his ministry, the local paper had carried a column reflecting on Malcolm Gladwell's recent book *Outliers*. Gladwell comments on the providential nature of most success, writing, "Nor is success simply the sum of the decisions and efforts we make on our own behalf. It is, rather, a gift. Outliers are those who have been given opportunities—and who have had the strength and presence of mind to seize them."[2] Gladwell is not a religious writer, but his analysis has a distinctly theological tone, and Paul thought Gladwell's notion fit him well.

Paul recognizes that he has been fortunate—he calls it "amazing grace"—to find himself in the right job at the right time. As he looks back on nearly forty years of stable, fruitful ministry, he adds, "The absence of trauma has been a great blessing." Paul recognizes that he has been given many gifts—in his life, his work, and even in the settings and circumstances for his ministries. More than anything else, however, he points out, "I have been blessed by several father figures who helped form and guide me in becoming the man and the minister I am."

It's not that he needed a father. Paul's own father was an electrician, a stable man who was "a good fifties father" and had had grown up poor and embraced conservative values, including a deep respect for the church. Paul remembers his father being emotionally reserved but available, maintaining a solid attitude of dependability with a graciously affirming spirit. In that secure environment, with a mother who was ambitious for his success and a trustworthy father for a role model, Paul believes he was able to construct a foundation of confidence with which to face the world. Even more important, he was given the gift of learning from a trusted other without feeling threatened or constrained. His relationship with his father, and then later with his much-appreciated father-in-law as well, taught him that we can learn from another even as we begin, with natural caution and inevitable missteps, to practice life on our own terms.

His first instructors in ministry were pastors in his childhood churches and chaplains and teachers in school. He learned the

basic skills of ministry in seminary, but he was even more profoundly shaped in those heady years by his growing friendship
with Guy. When Paul and Nona moved into the student-housing
complex, they quickly warmed to their new neighbors, Guy, an
African-American doctoral student, and his wife, Carrie. At first
Guy was an older brother, showing Paul the ropes of this new
life, but as the years went on, he became mentor and teacher and
eventually a peer and mutual admirer.

Guy recalls asking Paul to be his driver to a weekly teaching
assignment he had in a nearby city. Guy needed the help because
of his poor night vision, but he also wanted stimulating companionship on these late-night journeys. Guy now thinks that over
the course of those weekly two-hour drives together along dark
lonely roads, he became for Paul what he remembers Christian
educator Ross Snyder called an "adult guarantor." In that role,
according to Snyder, a person who has mastered the mystery of
being an adult conveys that mastery to another. Paul found in
Guy not only a supportive friend and wise advisor, but also a
lively collegial model for shared theological engagement with the
world. In the process Guy, who eventually enjoyed a long career
as a professor of congregational ministry at that seminary, not
only confirmed Paul's call to ministry but also granted him a sense
of blessing. The blessing was made explicit when Guy preached
Paul's installation sermon in his first ministry, "probably integrat-
ing that church for the first time," Paul says.

It was Sam, though, the senior minister with whom Paul
worked as a young associate in the first congregation he served,
who showed him the ways of the world of ministry and offered
a distinctive model of pastoral leadership for him. Sam had been
a successful trial lawyer and law professor before he sensed a call
to ministry and went to seminary (he says he "fell from law to
grace"). After his first ministry in a very small parish, Sam became
senior minister in a prestigious church where he refused to be installed until the congregation had called Paul as associate, so they
could be installed together. "We were as different temperamentally
as we could be," Paul says, "and yet we became an incredibly effective team." Paul admired Sam's more aggressive approach, once

demonstrated in a board meeting. A prominent elder was trying to force the church to take a particular action by threatening to withhold his pledge and leave. Sam simply said, "The church of Jesus Christ is not for sale, and we'll have your transfer papers ready for you in the church office in the morning." Paul sees himself as much less bold, a person who wears well over time, like a comfortable sport coat, but in Sam he came to see clearly the value of strength and prophetic witness.

Kelley, one of the several young ministers who have learned under Paul's tutelage, remembers him often telling stories about Sam that provided glimpses not only of the man, but also of high ideals for shared ministry. She still thinks of the "Shout for Joy" pendant, given to him by Sam, that Paul continues to wear on a chain around his neck over his liturgical robe every Sunday, and she thinks the image has become an icon through which Paul encounters his own joy in ministry. When she and Paul taught a course for new pastors on building an effective male–female pastoral team, it was abundantly clear to her that Paul had been well schooled in respectful collegiality in ministry. "Sam was one of the great blessings of my life," Paul says.

Paul also speaks admiringly of Sam's technical skills as a preacher and administrator, and he's grateful for his generosity in accepting this young just-out-of-seminary idealist into a truly shared ministry. Although he was a good youth minister, Paul recalls being not a very good preacher at first. But Sam somehow kept opening doors of opportunity to him and giving him encouraging feedback that allowed him to grow. After a time, he and Sam were regularly sharing preaching duties, often dividing the sermon fairly equally in a shared format that gave each of them visibility in the pulpit.

But he especially recalls Sam's practical guidance about facets of ministry that weren't covered in the seminary curriculum—such as temptation. Paul vividly recalls the time, in the midst of a conversation about his work with some of the women volunteers in the parish, when Sam looked him in the eye and said, "Paul, there are some women who just like a man in uniform. Sometimes they'll come after you. Don't flatter yourself that it's about you. You need to protect yourself." In later training in pastoral counseling, Paul came to understand more completely the nature of transference, and as gender-justice issues were more fully recognized through reports over the years of too-frequent pastoral misconduct, Paul has become keenly aware that it is the minister's own power and boundaries that must be managed. So even though the teaching may sometimes have needed to be reinterpreted, he has not forgotten the practical wisdom of his mentor—and he guards carefully against his own temptations.

Paul thinks Sam was way ahead of his time in destroying the "imperial pastor" model and demonstrating there is no need for a top dog or an only dog. He recalls fondly Sam's habit of coming into his office and "plopping down on the sofa for a chat." He wonders if they may have sometimes been too wasteful of time in such relaxed conversations, but he continues to follow Sam's example in his own practice as head of staff. And his old friend Guy, after more than thirty years of seminary teaching, asserts, "If young ministers could have more long times of seasoning with people like Sam, who were as good at being pastors and as generous with pastoral responsibilities, we'd have a different and more lively church today." Guy's research for the Board of Ministry of his denomination has confirmed how important it is for young ministers to have such time and attention and encouragement to claim their gifts.

PASTORS NEED COMPANIONS

Ed helped organize his first peer support group as a brand-new associate minister in his first parish out of seminary. He invited other younger clergy in the community to meet together for coffee and conversation once a month, rotating their meetings among their various churches. As a seminarian, he had learned the value of such groups in pastoral counseling classes and CPE, and his need for such a group became especially urgent when his senior pastor announced his resignation just a few months after Ed arrived at the church. The group talked about social justice (it was the seventies, after all, and most were mainline pastors), and they shared with one another the usual complaints of clergy—demanding parishioners, inadequate compensation, the need to find time for both ministry and family. But they also talked of their personal struggles in faith, challenged each other about theology and the practice of ministry, and even took an overnight retreat to exchange life stories. For the next forty years, until he retired, Ed repeatedly pulled together such peer groups wherever he went, supplementing that support system with a deeply intimate relationship with his wife and occasional relationships with a therapist or a spiritual director. "I am convinced I would not have been a very good minister, and maybe not even stayed in ministry, if it had not been for those relationships over the years," Ed says. "Jesus had his disciples, and pastors need companions as well to sit around the fire and gripe and dream and occasionally weep."

A generous mentor

While Paul learned skills and strength and self-restraint from his mentor in ministry, he also learned about mentoring from Sam. And he's taken that learning to heart. Paul has come to understand that his pastoral leadership is not only about the guidance and care he provides to the parish; that it is also, perhaps even more significantly, about the training he provides to his colleagues in ministry and to his parish leaders.

Like his biblical namesake, Paul recognized early on that his ministry would be enriched and even extended by associations with modern-day Barnabases and Silases and Timothys—and yes, also Phoebes and Nymphas and Marys whose stories of vital ministry are neglected in Scripture. And like the biblical Paul, he has found that those relationships sometimes involved tensions and inevitably led to separate journeys so that the gospel might be spread. But seeds of ministry were sown, and young clergy were nurtured in his tender care.

Paul seems to have taken Jesus's parable about the seed sown on rocky ground, among thorns, and upon good soil to have particular relevance for his calling as a mentor to his younger colleagues.

After all, if he can cultivate bountiful fruit in his own parish, how much more can be grown and harvested through multiple programs in a growing church and even in several well-tended churches? As the parable says, seed sown in good soil bears fruit thirty, sixty, and a hundredfold.

"I really like being a mentor and supporting those being called into ministry," Paul notes. "I see their successes as my success." He is keenly aware of being a role model to these younger colleagues, so he seeks to be transparent, freely sharing ambitions, disappointments, and especially uncertainties. He gives particular attention to treating others with the respect he was shown in his own maturation.

Recalling the generosity with which Paul entrusted responsibilities to her when she was a young associate pastor of First Church more than fifteen years ago, Kelley remembers with particular gratitude the opportunity Paul gave her to preach on a Christmas Eve and to be in charge of an important elders' retreat. Experiences like these were repeated throughout her years at First Church, leveraging personal affirmation into a growing confidence in her own ministerial gifts. When I mentioned to Kelley that this year Paul invited one of his current associates to preach on Easter Sunday, she observed through welling tears, "That's servant leadership."

James Kouzes and Barry Posner in their classic guide to effective leadership, *The Leadership Challenge,* cite a study on corporate innovation among high-achieving companies which found that "trust was 'the number one differentiator' between the top 20 percent of companies surveyed and the bottom 20 percent. The top performers trust empowered individuals to turn strategic aims into reality. The more trusted people feel, the better they innovate."[3] Mentoring younger leaders by entrusting them with responsibility for their own fields of work, as Paul has done so well, builds trust and fosters vitality in the church.

Russell, a senior human-resources officer in a large health-care system, agreed to chair the church's personnel committee after his own experience of receiving Paul's pastoral care through a difficult personal situation. He saw not only Paul's skills as a pastor but also his need for support in coordinating and guiding his staff as he juggled several different hats—CEO with lay leaders; shepherd, teacher, and even counselor with all staff; pastor to people in the parish; and husband and father. Russell believes that one of Paul's greatest strengths is his willingness to recruit strong staff people who take care of their own areas of work, combined with his certainty that he does not need to be in charge of everything. And as an HR specialist, Russell knows the other major finding from the Kouzes and Posner work is that "people who are trusting are more likely to be happy and psychologically adjusted than those who view the world with suspicion and disrespect."[4]

So the fruitfulness of Paul's ministry begins with *entrusting* gifted people to develop and use their own gifts. Such trust is the foundation of all faithful practice, beginning with Abram's radical willingness to gather all he owned and leave the familiarity of Haran to trek into the unknown of Canaan, and continuing through Jesus's invitation to "Believe in God, believe also in me." Thirty-seven of the Psalms center on the importance of trust in our relationship with God, while God's willingness to trust humankind is emphasized from the stories of Moses through that great cloud of God's leaders who have been entrusted with God's word and work through the ages.

God's entrusting nature is a primary model for godly living, and trust certainly must be incorporated into effective pastoral leadership. Jethro advised his son-in-law Moses that he couldn't possibly take care of all of the people of Israel in the wilderness, and so he should appoint assistants to listen to the people's complaints. Jesus knew he couldn't do his earthly ministry by himself, so he called twelve followers to be his close companions, and he sent them out to the surrounding towns to spread the Good News. He must have been sure that these twelve weren't nearly the gifted messengers that he himself was, but he entrusted them with the job anyway. The early church appointed deacons to tend to the needs of the Hellenist widows, and Paul and Barnabas appointed elders in Antioch and "entrusted them to the Lord in whom they had come to believe" (Acts 14:23).

The risk of trusting others is so important in pastoral leadership because it allows us to look beyond the limited gifts of the other with confidence in God's presence and power at work in and through the other. Paul and Barnabas entrusted the Antiochian elders "to the Lord," not only to their own human resources. When the contemporary Paul entrusts his associate ministers to preach on "high holy days," he knows that these young ministers may not yet have fully developed homiletic talents. But he also knows that God's word is more powerful and comes from somewhere deeper than a preacher's frail words.

Words and talents do matter, of course. So entrusting must be accompanied by *equipping*. Teaching and training have been central to Paul's practice of mentoring his colleagues in ministry, and he has employed several primary ways of equipping these saints for pastoral excellence, especially telling stories and modeling behavior.

"Sometimes they probably get tired of hearing my stories, but I tell them anyway," Paul says, affirming his belief in the power of narrative. And it is clear from talking with his former staff members that they remember and learned from those oft-told stories. Kelley, for example, recalls with fondness the stories Paul told of being an associate himself and was able to extrapolate from those stories her own applications in ministry. Tom, who returned from a self-imposed exile from ministry by becoming an associate with Paul at First Church, delights in Paul's story of converting First Church's boardroom into a more egalitarian environment. When Paul came, the boardroom had a fancy table with a "king chair" with arms at the head of the table, along with two side chairs without arms for the associate ministers. It didn't take Paul long to replace the unequal chairs, so that the seating arrangements clearly conveyed a collegial ministry. Modeling the pastoral life was another way Paul equipped his colleagues for healthy ministry. Both Tom and Kelley cherish the example Paul set in not carrying the whole load by himself. They especially appreciate the way he set clear boundaries between his work life and his family life. Kelley says, "He was a different Paul at home with Nona and the girls from when he was on duty at church," and he took his vacation time and days off religiously. And Paul himself is very clear that giving priority to a stable and enriching marriage and family life, with a wife who is an emotional anchor for him, is a central reason he has been able to last in ministry. He values formal learning, of course, as his own regular participation in continuing-education events attests. But Paul knows that ministry is itself a lived story, built upon the models displayed in countless stories told in Scripture and literature and through lives revealed in current human experience. Russell, his HR lay leader, says Paul is probably not the best sermonizer there ever was, but sees in him great strengths in coaching younger staff and offering a balanced model of the well-lived pastoral life.

Out of this coherent base emerges a third dimension of his leadership: *encouraging*. Tom was the second son of a minister, but he resisted the call to ministry until his older brother died. He then embarked on a traditional path through seminary and into a couple of smaller churches until, in a difficult parish and a troubled marriage, he quit ministry and became a brewer to pay the bills. After a divorce and a remarriage he asked himself, "Is brewing beer what I want to do with my life?" The question led him back to serving as pastor of a small rural congregation, which he says "nursed me back to health." When First Church announced that it was looking for an associate, he thought he had no chance of being considered because of his detours in life and ministry. But he thinks Paul saw him as a bit of an outsider, a little unorthodox, and related to those qualities in himself. So he was called and accepted the invitation to be a colleague.

Tom recalls that a wise elder in the church told Paul, when First Church called Tom as associate, "You need a colleague, not someone to mentor." When Tom reflects on his years at First Church, he remembers that he was more an equal colleague in ministry than an eager apprentice. But now, as Tom talks about his own role as pastor of a medium-size thriving congregation, it is clear that he has incorporated into his ministry many of the examples Paul modeled. More important, Tom's renewal of confidence in his call and his more mature perspective on the work of ministry is shaped largely by the example and the encouragement that Paul offered him in their years of working together, and still offers to him as a fellow pastor in the community.

Kathy, who had been church shopping when Paul came to be pastor at First Church, found new hope in the congregation as Paul's ministry began. She quickly came to appreciate his open and approachable style, saying he was "not overly impressed with himself—very human and not afraid to let it show." She treasures his pastoral gifts, recalling with some emotion his care for her father when he was dying, including his knowing when to overrule the surgeon's dismissal of the need for prayer and Paul's way of "dealing with Daddy matter-of-factly when he was hallucinating." But she particularly admires his ability to develop a strong staff whose members respect one another and let others have their say. She experienced that herself at the first church board meeting she attended when it took forever to get through the minutes of the previous meeting. She suggested to Paul that they begin to use a "consent agenda," and he immediately said, "Wow, we're going to try that." And it worked. As a laywoman in the church, she felt his encouragement and saw the positive results.

Mentoring becomes blessing

Why not just call Paul a mentor? That's the term, after all, that has increasingly been used in our culture for everything from volunteer "big brothers" and "big sisters" who take children under their wings to formal or informal role models at work. Mentors teach and guide; they entrust, equip, and encourage. And they are important people in our lives. As families have become more fragmented in our culture, we have come to see how very important mentors are to children. The important role of mentors in helping to shape professionals of various kinds is also much more widely recognized now. Or, if we think the term *mentor* is overused, we could describe Paul with some more technical phrase like Ross Snyder's "adult guarantor." He has surely mastered the mysteries of ministry, and he has guided a number of younger clergy into that mysterious realm.

But the term *blessing* goes much deeper than teaching or coaching. Talking these days with Kelley and Russell, Kathy and Tom, one cannot help noticing the depth of their appreciation for Paul as a pastoral leader, just as Paul shows deep appreciation for Guy and Sam. He is more than a mentor to them, although he is surely that. I think Paul has become, quite unselfconsciously, an agent of blessing to those with whom he works.

Blessing is soul work, touching the depths of another's being to assure someone that he or she is loved at the very core. Blessing may also affirm capability, as Kelley experienced when Paul entrusted her with important tasks. To bless is to bestow enduring affirmation on another, and one who receives such blessing is changed forever. Blessing is a spiritual transaction, and while blessings may be sought in formal, ritualistic fashion (confessing "Bless me, Father, for I have sinned" or "asking the blessing" before a meal), it is experienced with greater impact when it comes unbidden, in spontaneous and sometimes surprising ways. Blessing may be conveyed through such simple gestures as telling stories openly while plopped on the couch, sharing beers at the end of a difficult meeting, and trusting an inexperienced minister.

Paul was blessed by his father, that quietly affirming electrician who fostered the basic security of which Erik Erikson speaks in describing the well-formed personality. He was blessed by Sam, his mentor in ministry in that first parish out of seminary, and he carefully translated Sam's advice and applied it to his own situation, hearing Sam's stories and creating some new ones of his own. Relationships such as these, as well as those with Guy and his father-in-law and several others, amplified by some mysterious power—call it grace—have bestowed upon Paul this sense of blessing. He, in turn, has nurtured it in his own family and work and harvested that seed to replant in the lives of others.

Kathy says that Paul's ministry is "incarnational, that God is present in how he is with folks. Sometimes he is frustrated and impatient, like God must also be, but he manages to lead through that, because he loves people." Kathy's analysis was made explicit by a young father whom Paul visited just after this young couple's baby was born dead. "It was the first dead baby I'd ever held and baptized," Paul recalls, "and when I walked into the room and the dad told me what had happened, I grabbed him and said, 'Oh, shit!' I wanted to run from that room, and all I had was 'Oh, shit!' and some prayers." But some months later, the young father wrote Paul and said, "Paul, you were Jesus Christ to us that day. Your expletive was the only truthful thing said that day. That you stayed there with us was enormous."

Tom believes that Paul has strengthened First Church immeasurably by broadening the base of the church's leadership. On a personal level, though, Tom experienced his relationship with Paul as a blessing in his life which he now perceives as a mutual blessing in their shared ministries in different congregations. Kelley is grateful for the self-confidence she continues to enjoy after sharing ministry with Paul, and she translates this gift into "a more peaceful presence" in her current life and ministry. She also finds Paul's stories and maxims springing spontaneously into her days, like her recollection of his answer to her question about how to receive gifts. "You just say thank you," he told her. And so she does, to Paul's gifts and God's.

Kelley's gratitude is a way of living into her own blessedness. Psychology calls this process the development of self-esteem, or ego strength. One who receives and lives into the blessings of his or her life brings resilience to face hardships. The person who recognizes and integrates blessing develops a reservoir of capacity for achieving his or her potential. Each small blessing builds upon the one before, allowing a person to withstand the challenges and even curses that inevitably come in life. Self-esteem transformed into blessing puts down deep roots into the soul's core.

Leaders who incorporate their own blessedness into their ministries can transform the lives of individuals as well as the congregations they serve. In his insightful book *Becoming a Blessed Church,* Graham Standish has set forth a compelling vision of how a congregation of believers might become a truly blessed community, a group within which people may experience and offer blessing to one another and to the world. Standish says that at its core, blessedness means "living and leading in such a way that God's purpose and power flow through everything."[5]

After describing his model of a "blessed church," Standish goes an important step further to describe the qualities that best enable leaders to guide a congregation to such blessedness. These leaders, says Standish, have become "trusting, encouraging, compassionate, visionary, able to articulate that vision, sacrificially selfless, and committed to outreach."[6] Notice that he does not say they are pious or charismatic or that they are fully trained in the Seven Habits of Highly Successful Leaders (although probably none of those qualities would hurt). Rather, leaders who bless are those who stand with their colleagues in dedicated, collegial, humble, and hopeful ways. For Paul, that means that he is not thinking, "I'm going to be your mentor, but simply thinking about staff as 'we.'"

Most of all, leaders who guide their colleagues and their churches to become communities of blessing are those who recognize that their gifts and their calling come from somewhere beyond themselves. As Sam says, "Paul sees the divinity of his calling." Leaders like Paul realize that they are agents of something beyond themselves, not in some grandiose, messianic way, but as servants of that greater power. They come to see, perhaps not at first but over time, that they have themselves been blessed in countless ways, big and small, and out of that wealth of blessing they are able to share blessing with others.

As he approaches his fortieth year of ministry, Paul understands quite well that his blessings, and his blessed life, are all gifts. And what's more, he knows that he is among the servants who received a larger portion of talents, so he feels a particular responsibility to invest those talents well. "God has blessed me, and I need to continue to recognize that—and to remind myself that it's not about me, and that can be a bit of a struggle for me. But I treasure the respect and friendship of these younger colleagues." Talking with Kelley and Russell, Kathy and Tom, it seems he has invested well. The fruits of his ministry are multiplying.

chapter 9

Pathways to Leadership that Lasts

The men and women in these stories I've told about fruitful pastoral leaders have not only been faithful stewards of the talents they have been given; their leadership will also have lasting impact in the lives of people, congregations, and communities. None of them provides a universal model for effective ministry, of course. All have carried out their diverse ministries in ways congruent with their own personalities, their skills, and the distinctive situations in which they have been called to serve. Fruit is always grown and harvested locally, after all, and the leadership these pastors have offered and the results of their work are no exception.

I do think, though, that we can extract from their stories some common factors in the ways they have exercised their ministries— and these are crucial contributions to the enduring effects of their work. These recurrent behaviors, beliefs, and practices, taken together, form a distinctive pattern that seems to undergird long-lasting ministry. As we seek to heed Jesus's call to bear fruit that lasts, I believe that these elements for enduring excellence are essential pathways for pastoral leadership that has lasting positive consequences. Excellent pastors inevitably have specific skills in ministry that contribute to their effectiveness. Being an engaging preacher, providing sensitive pastoral care to members, running effective meetings, conducting lively worship services, teaching interesting classes—skills like these are central to pastoral success. Beneath these skills, however, are the more important qualities of personality and practice of leadership that foster enduring transformation. Such leadership may take different forms in each situation, of course, and the relative prominence of the elements in the seven stories I've told here varies. But the pattern of pastoral leadership that characterizes such pastors always seems to include at least the following seven elements:

- They feel called to *holy purpose.*
- They are *dependably authentic.*
- They nurture *trusting relationships.*
- They live as *generous servants.*
- They have been *creatively adaptable.*
- They display *disciplined persistence.*
- They practice *faithful spirituality.*

While it is certainly possible to be an effective leader and exhibit only some of these characteristics, the ministers described in this book demonstrate that these seven paths offer the best hope for practicing pastoral leadership that produces enduring results.

Such excellence, like all sound ministry, begins with a vision for the future coupled with clarity about the minister's own role in leading people toward that future. Clarity of purpose is the first pathway of fruitful pastoral leadership.

WHY NOT ME, TOO?

Nadine didn't really set out to be a pastor, but she certainly had the experience and even the bloodlines for faithful religious leadership. Her parents were both active lay leaders in her small-town church, and one of her ancestors was a widely known hymn writer. She had seen good ministry in action. After college she married a pastor, and she helped him in the parish while raising their two children. She faced some day-to-day challenges exercising leadership in the church in

a time before women went to seminary and when ordination of women was still a rarity. But when illness disabled her
minister husband, Nadine stepped into his ministry, and out
of necessity launched her own career as a minister in both
congregation and judicatory. She had only an undergraduate
degree in religion, but her denomination eventually recognized her call and found a way for her to be ordained. "I don't
think anyone laid hands on Mary or Martha or Lydia or those
other women in the Bible," she points out, "but they were
engaged in powerful ministries and were some of the first
Christian leaders. Why not me, too?"

Holy purpose

Vision and purpose go hand in hand. Vision is born of imagination, an ability to see beyond present circumstances and resources.
Through deft skill, determined force of will, and persuasion, often
leavened by heroic courage, leaders engage those around them in
the pursuit of an ideal, invigorating people and organizations in
ways that bring to life that which began as a mere idea in the
leader's mind. Vision is the birthplace of purpose.

Visionary leaders are quick to wonder, "What would it be like
if . . . ," and then to invite others to explore that unknown land.
Vision like this is fueled by inspiration, and to whatever extent the
spirit we inhale is in some sense holy, it clearly comes from somewhere deep within or far beyond ourselves and propels us into a
different place. Therefore, the leader's attentiveness, whether to
the still small voice within or to the unarticulated dreams of those
surrounding her, is a necessary component of vision.

Purposeful leaders do not merely react to immediate challenges
with short-term solutions. Such reactive leadership too easily becomes frantic, turning first one way and then another to defend
against threats that pop up like obstacles in a video game. Reactive
leaders forfeit agency for defensiveness. Leaders driven by a sense
of purpose, on the other hand, never lose sight of mission. The
word *respond*, in fact, comes from the Latin root for "promise."

To respond is to recommit to the original promise, to take action that ensures faithfulness to purpose. Responsive leaders listen with one ear to the urgent ringing of alarms while keeping the other ear attuned to the deeper hum of mission. Certainly these leaders must address crises as they arise, but they refuse to be distracted from larger principles by momentary demands, no matter how urgent or frightening. Leaders fueled by clarity of purpose know and can articulate their mission in both succinct and compelling fashion.

Trey, whose story is told in chapter 5, embraced early in his life a vision for a more just society. Fueled by that vision, he has worked in determined fashion to implement it throughout his ministry. This work became his purpose. Much of the practical work to which he has devoted his ministry—building affordable housing for the poor and providing food for the hungry, for example—could have been carried out by any good social worker or community organizer. But Trey understood this work as "advancing the reign of Christ on earth," a perspective inspired by the preacher he heard as a teenager and then deepened by Dr. Martin Luther King Jr.'s "powerfully prophetic voice for God's intentions for America."

Trey had not grown up in a religious home, although he recalls his mother as being quite socially progressive, so the values of social justice he embraced were familiar to him from childhood. But his dedication to *holy purpose* emerged from his exposure to religious teachings in church, combined with his own growing sense of God's presence and call in his life. In college and seminary he developed a theological perspective and a language to interpret this work, and he began to practice spiritual disciplines and to cultivate collegial relationships that strengthened his religious understanding of his call. Trey's own pilgrimage, then, provided a model for Kip, one of his current parishioners, who has seen and embraced through Trey's example new spiritual dimensions to his own longstanding commitments to social justice.

Although I see Trey as a man of holy purpose, he and the other pastoral leaders whose stories I have told in this book would be uncomfortable hearing themselves described as holy men or women. They would readily acknowledge they are saints only in the sense that the apostle Paul uses the term to refer to all Christians. Besides, all of them can be decidedly impious on occasion. But when I speak of "holy purpose" here, I use the term "holy" in a way similar to Episcopal priest and seminary teacher Margaret Guenther's description of spiritual direction as "holy listening."[1] Guenther suggests that what makes the listening distinctively holy is not just the attitude of gracious hospitality and hopeful encouragement that the listener brings to the encounter. These qualities might just as easily be found in a caring therapist or even a good friend. What makes the listening holy is the explicit focus on and trust in God's activity in the life of the other as well as in the encounter itself. Similarly, then, anyone can organize his or her life around lofty purpose. That purpose becomes *holy*, however, not only because of the high values prized and the goals pursued. The distinctiveness grows out of a keen awareness of divine presence perceived at the very core of one's existence along with a confident hope in the transformative power of God.

Such holy purpose may be born in a mystical encounter, like my own experience of sensing a Samuel-like call in a night of prayer while attending a summer church camp in high school. Or it might emerge in more gradual and less dramatic fashion, as it has for many. It could be formalized in a process of ordination, although a sense of divine call is not reserved for clergy alone. The focus of such a call may be broad, like a call to being a parish pastor, or it may be quite specific, like Sue's sense of call to a specialized ministry of spiritual revitalization working with clergy. The focus of vocation may shift over time, and its urgency may wax and wane throughout the years of ministry. It is not uncommon for pastors, including some of those described in this book, to question their call at some point, and both clergy and laypeople may find truly holy purpose in less traditionally "religious" work.

Devotion to holy purpose can sometimes be dangerous. The 9/11 Islamic terrorists and the Christian crusaders of the Middle Ages both claimed holy purpose, which led to bloody slaughter. Holy purpose can easily become zealotry, as Wake Forest professor Charles Kimball has warned in his book *When Religion Becomes Evil*.[2] Although religion is not the only fuel that fires fanatics, it often becomes the foundation of such twisted devotion because of some adherents' misguided claims to absolute truth and demands for unquestioning obedience. A sense of holy purpose can be the source of sustaining energy and life-giving power only when it is surrounded by positive values. It must never be egocentric but must seek the common good. In her 2010 commencement speech at Smith College, television commentator Rachel Maddow noted this difference:

> Gunning not just for personal triumph for yourself but for durable achievement to be proud of for life is the difference between winning things and leadership. . . . It's agreeing that you are part of something, taking as your baseline that you will not seek to reach your own goals by stepping on the neck of your community.[3]

Maddow's advice to these future leaders in this competitive, materialistic society corresponds to the practice of the early Christian community, which "had all things in common," and it is consistent with the words of a different speaker two thousand years earlier who urged disciples to "love your neighbor as yourself."

Pastoral leaders who draw upon such motivation for themselves and who convey a compelling vision for such purpose to their colleagues and followers offer inspiration for enduring positive transformation. When holy purpose is surrounded by the other six characteristics of effective pastoral leaders, the potential for "bearing fruit that lasts" is enhanced. And when that purpose is clearly understood and fully integrated into the identity of the pastor, as the commitment to "advancing Christ's reign" has been for Trey, it becomes a crucial component for the authentic exercise of visionary ministry.

Dependable authenticity

Authenticity in ministry has been especially well described by the late Rabbi Edwin Friedman, beginning in his watershed book *Generation to Generation*. Drawing upon the systems psychology of Murray Bowen, among others, Friedman lucidly underscored the importance of what he called "self-differentiation" in the practice of ministry. By his use of that term, Friedman was emphasizing the fundamental significance of maintaining clear individual agency and firm human boundaries as a means to fostering healthy relationships and organizations. To exercise such self-differentiation, Friedman believed, one had to understand and live out of one's true self and had to engage others and the world with sure and consistent self-confidence.

Authenticity is being who you really are, as fully and appropriately as possible. To be authentic is to recognize that we all have many aspects of self, just as a gemstone has multiple facets. For the apostle Paul, authenticity meant acknowledging the inner struggle between that which he wanted and that which he hated. For the psychologist Carl Jung, it was recognizing that the *persona* an individual wears for the world masks the *shadow*, which is hidden from the world, and yet both are aspects of the whole self. Living with authenticity is to acknowledge that we are all complex beings who work to be in the world as honestly as possible, restraining in appropriate ways those parts of ourselves that may interfere with chosen purpose.

Parker Palmer has written eloquently about what it means to live an authentic life. In his work as a teacher and trainer of leaders, he has passionately encouraged people to live "whole" lives that bring into harmony the inner and the outer life. This theme is powerfully developed in his book *A Hidden Wholeness*, in which he calls upon his readers to listen to their inner voice and to risk sharing with others the true self that is the source of that voice. Palmer sees this work as soulful, based in an integrity that is the foundation of true authenticity and trusting community.

Carole's path of ministry (chapter 6) clearly reveals this *dependable authenticity*. Her calm engagement with the crisis-habituated St. Thomas parish helped members become calmer themselves, enabling them to discover and better employ their own resources. Carole's assistant noted, "She is centered within herself—she knows who she is, both good and bad." No doubt a significant source of Carole's authenticity has been her lifelong attention to becoming aware of who she really is, a process enhanced by her engagement in regular spiritual direction and psychotherapy and participation in supportive peer groups. Her deep spirituality and strong pastoral identity are also vital components of Carole's non-anxious approach to ministry, which has worked to build a more trustful and faithful community of believers.

Richard (chapter 2) also exemplifies this genuineness in the service of mission rooted in a lifelong comfort in his own skin. Richard's clergy colleague describes him as a person who conveys "I am who I am," and Julie, one of his parishioners, says he is "always consistent, always the same." Richard himself is keenly aware of the importance of being "just Richard," despite the honors and titles he has received over forty years of ministry. He traces that authenticity to the loving and stable family from which he came and the solid values with which he was raised and that still consistently guide his actions.

Brian, a pastor who, like Richard and Carole, has wrestled with the invitation to accept higher office in the church, explains why he declined to stand for election as a bishop:

> A friend advised me that one's relationship with people changes—it becomes broader and more shallow. I don't want to be idolized, and so I made a decision for authenticity. In my letter to my parish telling them I had declined the invitation, I said, "I intend to go more deeply with you."

In wrestling with the invitation to consider becoming a bishop, Brian came to understand that he is fundamentally a person who wants to be in genuinely authentic relationship with people—and he decided to live out that identity more fully.

Being consistently real is not enough to bring positive change, however. Some people's consistency may even be lazy or mean or dishonest. That's one reason why the other six characteristics of fruitful pastoral leadership must go hand in hand with authenticity. For Richard, dependable authenticity includes a steady kindness and coherent moral clarity that is understood by many as integrity. Likewise, Carole's ability to be "a truth speaker," as her parishioner Ettajane put it, is a vital trait, emphasizing the fundamental honesty that characterizes her relationships with others.

Business leader, author, and consultant Bill George talks of this idea of authenticity in his book *Authentic Leadership*. Writing to encourage business leaders to forgo short-term profit for long-term gain, George speaks of authentic leaders as those whose lives show that they are "understanding their purpose; practicing solid values; leading with heart; establishing connected relationships; and demonstrating self-discipline."[4] Dependable authenticity can never stand alone. It must always be accompanied by values and behaviors such as those George has listed or the ones I have described as the seven essential pathways of lasting pastoral leadership. Creativity and adaptability, for example, are valuable guards against an excessive dependability that hardens into stubborn rigidity. Likewise, loving concern for others and an attitude of humble service are antidotes against a boastful self-centeredness that could emerge from an extreme preoccupation with authentic self-disclosure.

Paul's letter to the Romans and his first letter to the Corinthians show the most fundamentally important way for Christians to guard against such self-defeating errors. The apostle properly grounds his true self in God's reliable providence. "Let the one who boasts, boast in the Lord" (1 Cor. 1:31), Paul reminds his readers, harkening back to the prophet Jeremiah's warning not to brag about one's own resources but in the steadfastness of the Lord. The most powerful source of the authenticity displayed by good pastoral leaders, then, is their confidence in God's loving and redemptive creation as the foundation of their worth and work. And the most visible expression of that authenticity, as well as one significant and readily available resource for shaping and sustaining it, is the lovingly honest connection that these leaders share with others in their lives.

Trusting relationships

Paul's story (chapter 8) illustrates how important it is to nurture *trusting relationships* to both shape and sustain pastoral excellence. The most important relationships for Paul were initially those with several father figures, including his own biological father, from whom he is clear he has received blessing. Guy, his mentor in seminary, and Sam, the affirming senior minister in Paul's first ministry out of school, modeled for him a genuine depth of sharing and collegial friendship, and in the process developed within him a capacity to bless others. As a result, he has been able to pass on that blessing over the course of forty years of pastoral ministry and has frequently taken younger clergy under his wing, guiding and empowering them to develop their own gifts.

Paul has carefully protected the sanctity of time and relaxed openness with his wife and children, and with treasured friends. Guarding and nurturing those relationships has been a chief way he has kept his own energies fueled so that he can be available for sincere connection with parishioners and colleagues. The family's cabin in the nearby mountains provides a sanctuary for times of refreshment and candid conversation about the challenges of life. As he nears retirement, he has also found great satisfaction in meeting monthly with a group of men of a similar age with whom he can share honestly about preparation and transition into a new chapter of life.

These relationships, both professional and personal, are a significant part of what has made it possible for Paul to be fully present as an effective pastor with members of his congregations over the years. His parishioner Kathy's touching recollection of his open relational style with her in conducting the business of the church and in his pastoral care of her dying father attests to Paul's ability to create loving connections in his ministry. And the stark authenticity of his visceral reaction in a hospital visit to the death of a baby was perceived by that father as a "truthful" embodiment of Christ's anguish at that tragedy. Paul's sincere and plainspoken connections with colleagues and congregants, learned from and supported by mentors, friends, and family members, have been the seedbed of his fruitful ministry out of which his pastoral skills have flowered. As Fred Craddock describes effective preachers: "The sermons and teaching become elevated because they are heard through the lens of the pastoral relationship."[5] If it is true, as some in his congregation have said, that Paul's greatest gift is not his preaching, Craddock's assessment explains the highly positive regard in which most of his members view him as their preacher.

For most ministers, formal or informal clergy peer groups are an accessible and effective means of growing in capacity for trusting relationships while also supporting and equipping participants for the work of ministry. Several of the pastors in this book have benefited from such groups, either facilitated by a designated leader or conducted by the participants themselves. The "Sustaining Pastoral Excellence" project of Lilly Endowment has underscored the importance of such peer groups, and a recent study conducted by Austin Presbyterian Seminary's College of Pastoral Leaders has confirmed the broader significance of such groups.[6] Janet Maykus and Penny Long Marler, coprincipal investigators for this research, found that participation in such groups fostered a feeling of renewal in ministry, had a positive impact on the pastor's relationship with family and friends, sparked greater creativity in the minister, and produced a greater sense of intimacy with God. Participation in peer groups also appeared to foster a richer "culture of involvement" in the congregations served by these pastors, bringing both greater numerical growth and deeper engagement with community service by the congregation. One of the key factors in clergy peer groups that positively correlated with these outcomes was a group culture that was cohesive, "like a family." Peer groups, it is clear, model and encourage pastors in the practice of nurturing relationships in their ministries.

It is important to note, however, that being well connected with others or grounded in a group of peers does not mean that the pastor loses his or her individuality. Dependable authenticity remains a necessary quality that helps pastors avoid becoming enmeshed in their families or their congregations. My friend Herbert Anderson, Lutheran pastoral theologian and author of several books about family ministries, used to talk about the challenge of being "separate together" in marriage. The most satisfying relationships, he was saying, are those in which each party is able to maintain his or her own integrity as they seek intimacy together. This principle of relationship is equally true for pastors in both their work and their personal lives.

One of the implications of this practice for maintaining authenticity is that support groups should not be composed only of "yes people." A climate of trust that fosters open disagreement and challenge in the group—"like a family," as the Maykus/Marler study found—is essential. Philip Amerson, president of Garrett-Evangelical Theological Seminary, underscores the importance of diversity in the membership of such groups. Pastors, he says, "need colleagues with whom they can have a sense of common cause, and also people who will push them and challenge them. And the really good pastors are those who don't limit that to other pastors—who value the laity who bring insights and resources from other realms."[7] Pastors who have the courage to risk genuine authenticity and who nurture open relationships with a wide range of people are more likely to find their own lives enriched and their ministries enhanced. Enduring leadership thrives out of such an environment.

The loving relationships that excellent pastoral leaders enjoy reflect mutuality: these pastors get and they give. Paul received mentoring from his father and other father figures, and he moved quite naturally into being a mentor for others. While we probably should not make too much of the fact that the seven pastors whose stories I've told in this book all grew up in stable families, I don't think that fact is insignificant. Not everyone who grows up in a stable family becomes successful or even well adjusted. And as countless examples will attest, people sometimes emerge out of horrible childhoods and chaotic families to become enormously effective. But there is ample psychological data to demonstrate that people who experience trusting relationships in their families growing up are often better equipped to engage in healthy positive relationships as adults. The ego strength with which they have been blessed allows them to be more generous in sharing their love and service with others.

Generous servants

Their own experience of being loved, then, allows these pastoral leaders to live their lives as *generous servants*. Richard's story (chapter 2) shows very well how being immersed in a milieu of generosity from childhood can lay the foundation for a life of servant leadership. His family's humble sincerity, shaped by cultural and religious values, gave birth to countless acts of giving and hospitality that have fostered in Richard a similar benevolence. His brother, Dennis, says Richard's kindness is incorrigible. He recalls that he gave Richard some much-needed tires for his car one Christmas and then learned a few weeks later that Richard had given the tires to someone who needed them more than he did. Dennis says of his brother: "If someone said they liked something he had, he gave it to them without thinking. 'Oh, take it,' he would say."

Richard gives himself away in leadership in much the same way. From his work as a missionary with the poorest of the poor in Peru to his demanding role as the chief administrative officer of the archdiocese during a time of great turmoil, and through his many years as pastor in parishes of diverse size and influence, Richard's consistent stance is that of a servant. He seldom says no to requests, although his disciplined self-care allows him to remain invigorated for his work. His parishioner Julie calls him "a welcoming spirit" and says that his work with people is "very respectful, always appreciative—he sets the tone for the whole parish. And his tone is about love and acceptance and servitude."

Richard is the epitome of servant leadership. The measure of his ministry is well described by Robert Greenleaf in his book *Servant Leadership*. Greenleaf asserts that true servant leaders help others grow, become more autonomous, and then become servants themselves, bringing tangible benefit to society's powerless and outcasts.[8] Richard's own care for others, but more important, his leadership of his parish and of the larger church, is always geared toward these ends—and the actions of his church's members bear witness to this result.

Being a servant does not necessarily go hand in hand with being a leader, of course, as many a hardworking minister would acknowledge. One of the most vivid depictions of a servant who, while a leader at one level, missed the opportunity to engage in servant leadership may be found in Kazuo Ishiguro's wonderful novel *The Remains of the Day*. Stevens, the English butler whose lifetime of service as the head of the serving staff of Darlington Hall forms the spine of the novel, dutifully serves his master through the years leading up to World War II. Suppressing emotion and even the promise of a romantic relationship in the service of what he considers the higher value of serving a great man, he is chagrined to realize too late that his employer has become, in the end, a Nazi collaborator and so has ushered in the decline of an era of nobility and grace. Toward the end of the novel, as Stevens tries to adjust to the ways of the new American owner of the great house, he attempts to relax his lifetime habit of austere servitude and learn to banter as Americans do. "After all, when one thinks about it," he says, "it is not such a foolish thing to indulge in—particularly if it is the case that in bantering lies the key to human warmth."[9]

What Stevens had lost in his dutiful service was his full humanity. He committed himself completely to a purpose that he understood to be appropriate for his station and skills, and he diligently performed his work with excellence. His leadership of the serving staff made him a role model for those workers. He was even generous in his dedication to his employer and to the standards of his profession. But he lost his soul as he confined himself to a narrow adherence to duty and the strictures of a fading and ultimately decadent culture. He stifled his own individuality, and he denied himself the joys of intimate relationship. Only near the end of his life did he begin to catch a glimpse of these deeper values as he gave himself over to learning how to banter.

Many loyal pastors who have given themselves generously to long lives of faithful ministry would recognize the costs and limitations of Stevens's servant life. Loyal service to people and to the standards of a profession is essential for the growth and maintenance of the church. Countless followers of Christ have faithfully served in such ways for centuries and so have extended the reign of Christ. These generous servants deserve to be celebrated. But the fruit of such service is greatly enhanced when accompanied by other characteristics of excellence in pastoral leadership, especially the gift of creativity, which emerges from sharing authenticity in warm human relationship.

Creative adaptability

"Ministry is as much art as it is science," says Sharon Watkins, general minister and president of the Christian Church (Disciples of Christ). "Done well, it combines skills and instincts and gifts, some of which can be taught and some of which emerge out of instinct and hard experience." She recalls her own early attempts to learn how to do ministry, and she remembers with amusement her first practice baptism—full immersion, as is the Disciples custom. "I had just graduated from Yale and was confronted with baptizing a woman as tall as I was. So I persuaded my friend Linda to put on a bathing suit and let me practice on her."[10] Out of her willingness as a young and inexperienced pastor to practice the skills of her profession in the safety of a friendship somehow came the capacity to lead a denomination and the opportunity to preach a powerful inauguration sermon to a president of the United States.

Performing an adult baptism by immersion without drowning the convert, or understanding the complexities of biblical criticism or even a church budget—these are skills that can be taught and practiced. Leading a neighborhood church's adjustment to serving an ethnically and economically changing neighborhood—truly adaptive change—requires more creative thinking and experimental action. Coping with a church's longstanding systemic conflicts, which may even scapegoat the minister, calls on the depths of a pastor's patience, insight, and resilience. Such pastoral challenges may require not only a significant deepening of those resources but also a creativity that envisions new possibilities for being church.

Christine (chapter 4) was one pastor who exercised extraordinary *creative adaptability*, drawing on a variety of coping skills as she endured a torturous few years of misery to reach a place where she could guide her congregation into greater health. After several years of nearly fatal illnesses and recurrent church conflict that occasionally turned vicious, she was ready to throw in the towel on this pastorate, and maybe on ministry itself. But by some mysterious combination of determined persistence, healing relationships, and divine providence, Christine survived that period and found herself and her church moving into a time of sustained fruitfulness. The congregation grew in size, relationships became more loving, and preaching and programs became more creative.

The key factors in Christine's leadership that helped produce these changes appear to be her innate "stress hardiness," her personal creativity, and her own spiritual revitalization. She herself was, first, an adaptable person who tried various ways of coping and leading before she finally found an approach that not only was genuine for her but also fit the congregation she was serving. That adaptability is surely part of her overall creativity. Her first career was as a musician, and she continues to be able to improvise and harmonize in her work as a pastoral leader. She would also acknowledge that the stressful times she endured deepened her spiritual life, taking her at times into realms of mystical inspiration that have strengthened her personally and enhanced her ministry.

Creative adaptability may be evident at any point during the course of a ministry, but it offers especially rich promise when it appears early in a pastor's career. Eight years ago, Matt became the youngest person ever ordained in his judicatory, and now he leads a dynamic five-hundred-member congregation that is the first new church start by his denomination in his midwestern city in more than one hundred years. Launched just four years ago, his is the fastest-growing parish in the judicatory—no doubt to the great surprise of many who resisted investing in this mission. The congregation is mainline to the core, but its vitality and rapid growth stand in stark contrast to many traditional city churches. On a recent Sunday, Matt preached on Mark's account of Jesus returning to his hometown of Nazareth, where he found only rejection. Matt's thoughtful and engaging sermon offered these words of hope: "Expectations shape the reality of our experience. Expecting little, Jesus's former neighbors received little. We must give God permission to surprise us!" Matt is keeping his eyes peeled for such surprises and is himself an agent in creating those surprises. He is well on his way toward becoming a pastoral leader who will "bear fruit that lasts," and he will surely do so if he persists in such creative work.

Disciplined persistence

One of my own role models for living with discipline was the late UCLA basketball coach John Wooden. When I was graduating from seminary and considering options for my first call, I was invited to interview with First Christian Church in Santa Monica, California, where Wooden was an elder. I remember that he was an usher on the Sunday I was there, quietly standing in the atrium and passing out bulletins and handshakes to worshipers as they arrived. A small-town Indiana boy, Wooden became one of the most successful college basketball coaches in history, leading his UCLA Bruins to a record eighty-eight straight victories and ten NCAA championships during a twelve-year span in the sixties and seventies. To be sure, he had recruited great players, and those were the days before the promise of big money and fame for pro careers lured players to cut short their college careers. But his life story and his coaching philosophy, combined with the demeanor I observed in church that Sunday and on televised UCLA games, indicate that his success was based in far more than access to raw talent. Coach Wooden was a remarkably disciplined man himself, and a key to his success as a coach was his determination to teach his young players the skills of a well-lived life. Core building blocks of that teaching (found in his famous "Pyramid of Success" lecture, delivered countless times in motivational speeches) were industriousness, self-control, conditioning, and patience.

John Wooden's coaching philosophy could surely have been applied to the teaching of young ministers—especially me, had I accepted the invitation to ministry in that church. Even though I went to another parish when I graduated from seminary, I continued to watch Wooden closely over the years, and not just because we both came from Indiana and I loved college basketball. He was clearly onto something, and his message to young athletes about *disciplined persistence* was as relevant to me and my colleagues in ministry as it was to the players he coached. And not surprisingly, considering Wooden's devout churchmanship, his philosophy was fundamentally grounded in core values of Christian faith and practice. Coach Wooden could surely have echoed, just before he died at age ninety-nine, the apostle Paul's words that that he had fought the good fight, finished the race, and kept the faith.

Russell (chapter 3) also knew how to live and lead with disciplined persistence. For more than forty years of ministry he brought to his work the same diligence that made him a long-distance runner well into his seventies. In the year of his seventy-eighth birthday he did another 10-kilometer run, and he felt so good when he finished it that he ran an additional 1.6 kilometers! Year after year, he called all his members on their birthdays, even after the membership reached two thousand. Sunday after Sunday he made sure that services lasted no more than one hour, so that the congregation could hold three services and still have time for fellowship between them. Summer after summer he went off to the Robert Schuller Institute to recharge his batteries and retool his mind. That disciplined determination allowed him to weather the difficult times at Faith Church and build it into one of the largest congregations in its synod. While many factors ranging from good genes to God's providence contributed to those results, none of Russell's accomplishments would have been possible without rigorous self-discipline and relentless commitment to thinking long term about his ministry.

The other pastoral leaders described in this book witness in their own ways to the importance of disciplined persistence. All have entered into long-term ministries. Trey speaks of "the view of the grandmother" in describing the importance of persistent dedication to addressing the needs of society. Richard religiously takes his apportioned time off for Sabbath rest, while Paul guards his family time and home space for refreshment from the demands of his work. Christine soldiered through the terrible conflict she found within her church to "transform the bricks" that now surround a healthier church because of her leadership. It's not just sticking around for the long haul that makes a difference, although that is significant. But it is also the disciplines of hard work, dedication to core values, and regular prayer that make a lasting difference.

Persistence can turn into stubbornness, of course. Holding on to ideas and goals that have outlived their time or were ill conceived in the first place is like placing new wine in old wineskins. Rigid thinking and unyielding opposition to change can stifle God's ongoing creation, as mainline American churches are too often finding. But determined commitment to high purpose that is well grounded in possibility and hard work is the executor of God's hope.

Disciplined persistence may be out of vogue in this age of instant gratification. When the explosive growth and contagious excitement of megachurches attract members and admiration for their apparent success, old-fashioned values like keeping one's nose to the grindstone can easily be neglected. Becoming a "one-minute manager" generates more attention than developing strategic plans for the next ten or twenty or one hundred years. But even Bill Hybels, the founding pastor of Willow Creek Church, outside Chicago in South Barrington, Illinois, has acknowledged that herding people into countless programs does not necessarily make them committed disciples. After documenting that new members who joined the church with enthusiasm were not staying active in the Christian life, Hybels has said, "We made a mistake. . . . We should have started telling people and teaching people that they have to take responsibility to become 'self-feeders.' We should have . . . taught people how to read their Bible between services, how to do spiritual practices much more aggressively on their own."[11] Disciplined persistence, in other words, is necessary for discipleship and is especially essential to continuing growth in faith.

Pastors must continue their own growth in faith and in leadership, just like laypeople. United Methodist bishop Janice Riggle Huie of Houston understands this need well, believing that pastors, including those in her Texas Annual Conference, must lead the way for the whole church to become lifelong learners. "Participation in a community of learning with enough depth to it would affect the culture of the . . . [church]. We have to help folks see themselves as lifelong learners and that the church is a community of lifelong learning."[12] Bishop Huie insists that this commitment by pastoral leaders to lifelong learning is more than learning new ideas or skills in continuing-education events, although such experiences are part of the process. While such technical education may be helpful, the real change for which she hopes is adaptive, a cultural shift in understanding and practicing faith that is both courageous and imaginative.

Faithful spirituality

I've finally begun to learn over the past twenty years about the importance of being more faithful in my own spiritual practice. My deepening started during a time when I found myself in a clinical depression, and my friend Bill invited me to go off to a monastery with him for a week of silence and prayer. As the ice melted on the Merrimac River next to our retreat house, my own depression dissolved amid the loving hospitality of the monks. From my first spiritual director, Bob, I began to learn *lectio divina*, and at last, in late middle age, my love affair with God sprang to passionate life. My ministry prior to that week of prayerful silence came more out of my head than my heart. My faith was strong and my ministry well grounded, but the spiritual disciplines I began to learn that week transformed my understanding of God's love and have become ingrained in my life ever since.

It was this sort of experience that led Sue (chapter 7) to the ministry of spiritual revitalization she now performs. Her holy purpose for many years has been to invite and guide pastors into deeper practice of *faithful spirituality*. As she has carried out this ministry, she has been careful to attend to her own spiritual disciplines. She knows very well how often clergy lose touch with their relationship with God. Many times in retreats, she has heard pastors tell of their own journeys from enthusiasm about their service to dryness and wavering faith. So she is persistent in extending her specialized ministry and in her own quest for continuing growth in faith.

Joel, my current spiritual director, once told me that love of God was a lot like a long-term marriage. It has moments of great passion but probably more times of day-to-day routine, sustained by confidence in the dependable mutuality of love and determination to see it through. Joel's comments were offered to reassure me as I told him how disappointed I was at that time that the fervor stirred up in that first retreat had waned. That's why spirituality must be practiced faithfully. It's the constant attentiveness to spiritual dimensions of life and the thoughtful exploration of Scripture and theology and devotional literature that sustain the spirit, just as communication and chores and even arguments sustain a marriage beyond romantic nights of dancing under the stars.

Brian has learned this pattern of waxing and waning well. After many years, two books, and an honorary doctorate given for his work in teaching and writing about spirituality, he found himself ready to move on from a primary focus on spirituality in his ministry. The contemplative center he created at St. Michael's Church remains a vital gathering and teaching place for contemplative prayer, but Brian is finding his own spirituality more commonplace these days, more incorporated into his daily life than expressed in separate settings and practices. As his lively congregation has grown and become more of a program church[13] than a smaller body of spiritual seekers, his focus of attention has shifted to developing leaders and building a stronger financial base for the church. Meanwhile he's content to acknowledge that he may not become "enlightened" through some formal process of spiritual passages; he's relinquished the role of guru and has declined to be a bishop. But it could be that his very abandonment of the formal spiritual quest is what opens the door to God's unfolding creativity. Lifelong learning and faithful spirituality sometimes emerge from such letting go.

While holy purpose is the starting point for fruitful pastoral leadership, faithful spirituality is the thread that ties all of the other characteristics together. Sometimes it appears in bright and elaborate patterns, calling attention to its beauty. At other times, its invisible strength holds together seams and keeps hems at their proper length. But vital spirituality, sustained through its seasons by faithful disciplines, gives depth to a pastor's authenticity and equips him or her for trusting relationships. Faithful spirituality can be the crucible of divine creativity and a shelter in the midst of ministry's storms. Practicing spiritual disciplines and maintaining a sense of deep gratitude for God's generous grace are the foundation of generous service and an inspiring reservoir for determined persistence.

Pastoral leadership that lasts is discovered by way of these seven pathways leading through the tangled vines and branches of holy service. These practices are seldom included in a seminary curriculum; rather, they are charisms, gifts of God. But that does not mean they cannot be taught or strengthened or intentionally expanded and sustained. Equipping pastors to travel these paths is the urgent task of the church, and we turn to that task in the next chapter.

chapter 10

Tending the Vineyard

Fruitfulness emerges from a wonderfully complicated environment. Even the garden that began with orderly planting in straight furrows soon spreads into lush complexity. The roots and vines, leaves and blossoms, offer nourishment and protection that yield, when blessed by tender care and the fortunes of sun and rain and tiny bees, a bountiful harvest. It is a long and venturesome process, this planting and cultivating and waiting, its lineage extending back to creation and its practice sustained by relentless endeavor, patient hope, and complex relationships.

Pastoral leadership that "bears fruit that lasts" has much in common with the verdant fruitfulness of garden, orchard, and vineyard. Paul seems to understand this well in the evocative words of his letter to the church at Colossae. The fruitful leader in that ancient town not far from Ephesus was Epaphras, "our beloved fellow servant." We know very little of this pastor's story, but through the apostle's commendations in Colossians (or perhaps it was Paul's disciple, if the letter was not written by Paul himself) and a brief mention in Paul's letter to Philemon, we do know something about the fruit he bore. The letter praises the fruitfulness of the church he served, evident in its loving good works and growth in knowledge of God, and it credits much of that result to the nurturance of Epaphras, who was in turn supported by Paul and Timothy. Epaphras's ministry with the Colossians was obviously a "turnaround" effort, guiding the church from a group that was "estranged and hostile in mind, doing evil deeds" (Col. 1:21) into a body clothed in a "new self, which is being renewed in knowledge" (Col. 3:10). The letter reminds the Colossians that a living faith must keep growing and being practiced. Faith in Christ, Paul points out, means patiently enduring challenges and fending off threats while supporting one another as brothers and sisters in order to continue to bear the gospel's good fruit. Finally, the letter promises that another faithful minister, Tychicus, is coming with their brother Onesimus to keep them connected with Paul and the larger community of believers, and to "encourage your hearts" (Col. 4:8). Future growth and harvests await!

The letter to the Colossians is a practical reminder that graceful and growing faith requires careful planting, strong connections, loving care, and nourishment from diverse resources. Likewise, pastoral leadership requires planting and connections and care and resources to "bear fruit that lasts." This milieu is the vineyard out of which fruitfulness emerges, and the whole church must protect and enrich that precious vineyard, as must individual pastors themselves. Caring for it is a shared responsibility as old as the first garden.

The ecology of ministry

Craig Dykstra, vice-president for religion at Lilly Endowment, talks of these connections and resources for cultivating fruitful pastoral leadership as components of the ecology of ministry. "Pastoral ministry is never the work of individuals in isolation," Dykstra explains. "The ecology of ministry comes out of a great historical web of ordered relationships shaped by the whole history and life of faith."[1] He points out that pastors begin to learn ministry in childhood and from their earliest experiences with communities of faith. While their understanding of ministry may be shaped significantly by a formal theological education and by the guiding structures of a judicatory, ministry continues to be formed by a wide range of connections throughout "the arc of learning over time." These experiences could include everything from mentoring, coaching, spiritual direction, and participation in peer groups of colleagues to engagement with the broader structures of society.

Most important, pastoral formation unfolds through the actual practice of ministry shared with communities of faith. It is this symbiotic process, Dykstra observes, out of which "pastoral imagination emerges over time and through the influence of many forces. It is always forged, however, in the midst of ministry itself, as pastors are shaped by time spent on the anvil of deep and sustained engagement in pastoral work."[2] Dykstra views pastoral imagination—this ability to see the reality of church and world in depth and to bring the pieces together with the gospel's transformative hope to create new reality—as an essential component of fruitful pastoral leadership that always goes hand in hand with "ecclesial imagination—a way of seeing the world through eyes of faith."[3]

Sharon Watkins, general minister and president of the Christian Church (Disciples of Christ), is one of a growing number of church leaders who see the wisdom of Dykstra's ecological vision of ministry, and she wants the task of forming pastoral leaders to be broadly shared in more creative ways. Out of her own rich pastoral imagination she says:

> Unfortunately, the church has ceded the responsibility of training ministers too much to the seminaries, but the church must be in better partnership with seminaries and other parachurch organizations in order to broaden and strengthen that work of preparation. We are in a time of transition, and everybody feels stretched, so it's a challenging time. The church is re-sorting itself.[4]

Brian McLaren, one of the leaders of the emerging church movement reaching across many denominations and evangelical nondenominational groups, echoes Watkins's assessment of "re-sorting," emphasizing that the needs of the modern church require a whole new set of skills that tap into human creativity to help people adapt to current needs. "These days," McLaren says, "you need to create space for people to ask their questions and explore for answers on their own. It's a very different set of leadership skills to create a learning environment, as opposed to indoctrination."[5]

Ecclesial initiatives, some imaginatively experimental, are emerging all across the country and responding to this broader understanding of needs and resources for the formation of effective pastoral leaders. Theological seminaries and judicatory leaders in particular are beginning to take concrete action to increase the partnerships and develop the resources that expand training beyond traditional academic settings. Dykstra points with admiration, for example, to the work of Virginia Theological Seminary, which has begun to focus additional attention and resources on the first three years out of seminary for new clergy, working in close partnership with parishes, judicatories, and specialists like mentors and coaches. In a similar vein, Philip Amerson, president of Garrett-Evangelical Theological Seminary, is especially pleased with that school's newly established "MDiv Plus" program, operating in partnership with Northwestern University's Kellogg School of Management to teach business and leadership skills to clergy, and with Samaritan Interfaith Counseling Service to provide coaching for recent seminary graduates. "We have pastors who know about the Bible or church history, but they don't know how to run a meeting or write a strategic plan or read a budget," Amerson says. He hopes this new program will provide a framework to help correct some of those deficits, and in the process help Garrett-Evangelical "move from being a seminary *of* the church to being a seminary *for* the church."[6]

Charles Crutchfield, United Methodist bishop of Arkansas, is working closely with his cabinet and congregational leaders throughout the area to provide training in advanced leadership skills that he believes are so desperately needed, coupling that training with a peer-support network called "Connected in Christ." He believes the pastors in his conference must move beyond their historic expectation about their relationship to the denomination—as he heard one pastor say, "I thought you guys were going to take care of me." He's working to develop among clergy in the state a greater sense of responsible autonomy in their own continuing formation along with a heightened sense of accountability to the church's mission and to their own ordination vows.[7]

Janice Riggle Huie, who preceded Crutchfield as bishop of Arkansas, where she launched that Connected in Christ program, now serves as bishop of the Houston Area (Texas Conference). She finds her interests being drawn to the challenge of "recruiting gifted and diverse young clergy and developing younger leadership."[8] My conversation with Bishop Huie came as she was returning from a youth academy, one of the places where she is investing her energies in the pressing task of developing younger leaders. "Their hearts are bent to mission, and their hearts are also bent to connectedness," she says, and she is eager to learn how the church can connect with this younger generation's interest in Facebook and similar avenues of learning and connection.

The stories of pastoral leaders told in this book reflect the importance of diverse resources in this wider ecology of ministry. Sue's ministry of spiritual revitalization (chapter 7), for example, brings connection with a faith-based counseling center and a community of monks to the continuing formation of clergy who come to her retreats. And now, as she is expanding that program to incorporate whole congregations into this process of spiritual development, pastors and congregations together are living out the vision of shared imagination and mutual ministry that Dykstra describes. Paul's practice throughout his ministry of mentoring younger pastors (chapter 8) shows very well the significance of both giving and receiving such continuing pastoral formation. All of the pastors I've written about in this book have expressed particular appreciation for peer groups, continuing-education experiences, counselors, and spiritual directors in their ongoing formation. The lasting fruit grown and harvested by these pastors has emerged from well-tended vineyards.

The particular ecology of these pastors' ministries illustrates the importance of strong connections and diverse resources out of which excellent ministry springs. Through their stories, combined with reports from academic settings, denominational leaders, and especially the significant discoveries emerging from projects being funded by the Lilly Endowment, four key elements are now coming to be recognized as imperative for the cultivation of enduring pastoral fruitfulness:

- Systemic commitment to lifelong learning.
- Intentional connection to communities of shared practice.
- Careful stewardship of the leader's own self.
- Strong roots and active exercise in a growing faith.

For pastors and for the church at large, the first of these elements, which undergirds the others, is a shared commitment to lifelong learning.

Lifelong learning

Dykstra's vision of the vineyard out of which fruitful pastoral leadership emerges is rooted in two thousand years of the church's history and extends across the many experiences of training and encouragement as well as life circumstances that may foster excellence in ministry. Although the seminary and the judicatory play key roles in this process of preparation and support, the church is increasingly recognizing that these two seminal institutions cannot do the job alone—nor should they. As Dykstra notes, "You don't become a doctor on the day you graduate from medical school."[9] Pastors must learn ministry as physicians and many other professionals learn their life's work, participating in internships and residencies that offer practice and encouragement and further opportunity for learning under wise supervision within the crucible of lived experience. What's more, this learning must be continuous throughout the minister's lifetime of service.

Bishop Huie of Houston emphasizes that this task of lifelong learning is much more than continuing to learn a few more pastoral skills in periodic continuing-education seminars. It is something much broader, necessitating a radical shift in the church's understanding of learning. She is focusing her efforts these days on deepening this continuing formation, so that it creates an environment in which the church's leaders may participate "in a community of learning with enough depth to it that it would affect the culture of the [annual] conference—helping folks see themselves as lifelong learners and that this [conference] is a community of lifelong learning."[10] This expanded understanding of pastoral formation would be the kind of adaptive change that Ron Heifetz at Harvard's Center for Public Leadership has described, going beyond mere technical adjustments focused on narrow issues or new skills. This transformation would require reimagining the process of ministerial education already shared by academic institutions and church structures, while also incorporating an acceptance and even an appreciation for "experiencing failure and learning to pick yourself up and dust yourself off," as Bishop Huie puts it.

John Wimmer, program officer with the Lilly Endowment, has seen overwhelming evidence of the value of lifelong learning for pastors in results from the sixty-three "Sustaining Pastoral Excellence" projects he has been overseeing for more than eight years. In those widely diverse programs he has witnessed the ways that effective leaders are adapting to changes in the world, and these innovative adaptations are underscoring for him the importance of understanding ministry as an intrinsically organic endeavor. "The pastor has to be a learner," he observes. "The congregation is going to change with every single step they take in advancing the ministry, so [pastors] have a new situation, a new congregation. If pastors have the right resources around them, then they have what they need to be able to continue to advance and bear increasing fruit."[11] Wimmer is clear, from his observation of many innovative projects, that pastors whose leadership brings the most effective change are those who are learning and growing themselves.

This commitment to lifelong learning, Wimmer has come to believe, is best implemented when the church encourages and supports as much "agency" as possible within pastors, allowing them the permission and freedom to act by their own inclinations and preferences"[12] while at the same time developing appropriate accountability to the church, to the pursuit of excellence in ministry, and to the core values of the gospel. "The more agency that is placed in the hands of pastors, and the more resources that are placed around pastors that respect that agency, the better able that pastor is to bear fruit over the long haul."[13]

The pastors described in this book have found various ways of exercising this agency while balancing it with a deep sense of accountability to their calls. Christine's creative adaptability (chapter 4) helped First Church over a period of twenty years move from a suspicious and even angry stance based in the members' woundedness from previous pastoral relationships to become a growing congregation with a deepening spiritual life and more active ministry to the community. The positive outcomes in this process seem to have been shaped largely by Christine's own determination to learn to deal effectively with the challenges she faced in leadership, drawing upon the resources of personal resilience, judicatory support, a supportive peer group, professional counseling and coaching, continuing-education experiences, and more disciplined personal spiritual practices. She exercised considerable agency, as Wimmer would say, and demonstrated a fierce commitment to learning what was needed. And she is still learning to this day, having recently begun a new coaching relationship to find help in managing the new administrative duties she has accepted.

Pastors who wish to bear fruit that lasts must claim this agency as an essential element of their call. In practical terms, and looking back at the seven pathways for enduring pastoral leadership defined in the previous chapter, claiming agency means that pastors must, for example, take the initiative to ensure that they are always refining their understanding of their fundamental purpose. This might mean writing or rewriting a personal mission statement or journaling about their unfolding discernment of God's call for their lives. Pastors who take agency seriously must also examine their own authenticity to make sure they are living out of their true self in ministry and sharing that self with the community of faith. This process could include seeking therapy to identify and integrate the various and sometimes conflicting voices within. *Agency* means that pastors must develop skills through seminars, coaching, and mentoring relationships that can help them respond creatively to the challenges they are facing in ministry. The point is this: primary responsibility for a commitment to constant learning rests with the pastor. It is part of the cost of call.

The responsibility for lifelong learning does not, however, rest on the pastor's shoulders alone. This must always be a shared burden with the larger church, and the church in all its manifestations must continue to provide abundant resources for the continuing formation of pastors. John Wimmer thinks one of the things this means is that judicatory and general-church officials and even congregational lay leaders should give both permission and encouragement to pastors to pursue greater self-direction. "Agency gets squelched by mechanistic bureaucratic practices and structures," Wimmer says. "Fruitfulness thrives when the right resources surround pastors and congregations to foster mutual agency and accountability."[14] This is not to say that all bureaucratic structures and responsibilities are bad. Brian McLaren's work with nondenominational churches has convinced him that some traditional structures, like a garden trellis on which a vine can grow and expand, provide a useful framework of support and accountability to guard against chaos. But the church's procedures and actions must always be crafted to foster, not stifle, fruitfulness.

Sharing responsibility for cultivating a community of lifelong learning is just one way that the church and its leaders must cooperate to ensure the proclamation and day-to-day enactment of the gospel. This is how ministry is practiced best—with mutual effort and expectant openness to God's continuing creation. For individual pastors, such mutuality and receptivity may be most accessible through active and self-conscious participation in small communities of shared practice.

RELATIONSHIPS ARE KEY

"The relational aspect of ministry is key," Judy says, as she thinks about what the church must be doing to support effective ministry in congregations. "In my own culture as a Native American, people are fundamentally relational, but I think that's probably true for every culture. If the relational piece of ministry could be foundational throughout the church, we would all benefit." Judy believes it has been opportunities for continuing education with colleagues that have made such a difference for her in her own ministry, and she wants the church to make more of those resources available to parish clergy. "The bureaucracy can be very confusing and some- times, especially for Native peoples, can foster alienation. Building strong relationships is essential for ministers, and for the church as well."

Communities of shared practice

Families are one kind of "community of shared practice." Chil- dren grow up in families learning core values and beliefs and ritu- als, and they internalize an understanding that "this is how our family does things." The influence of those traditions and evolving ideas and practices lasts for life. The church is a similar kind of community, one in which people are called to bear one another's burdens, to recognize how the varieties of gifts God has bestowed belong to the same body, and to encourage one another in wit- ness and service. These are some of the practices that members of the church are called to share. At its best, therefore, the church might be described as a diverse and growing community of shared practice, whether conceived internationally, denominationally, ec- umenically, or congregationally.

Richard (chapter 2) definitely learned how to be a pastor and a leader in both of these communities. Growing up, he observed and embraced the religious commitment and generous hospitality of his family, and the ideas he learned there continue to be reinforced and shaped by his ongoing connection to that faithful and loving family. He and his family still support one another in ministry and learn from one another what it means to be a Christian and a min- ister—ordained or not. His formation as a pastor, furthermore, came not only from his experience growing up in and continuing to be part of that family, but also through his education in semi- nary and his ministry experiences as a pastor, a missionary, and a judicatory official in the larger church. And he continues to share the practice of ministry with his colleagues in ministry and with the laypeople of Risen Savior Church.

Fruitful pastoral leaders understand the importance of being part of such communities, and they make sure they have regular continuing access to such groups. The most basic community of shared practice for Christians is, of course, the congregation. When the central relationship between pastor and congregation is working well, there will be reciprocal teaching and learning and encouraging and confronting as all seek to live out God's call in their lives. Carole's ministry (chapter 6), for example, shows how both she and the members of her congregation have learned and grown with one another to become more confidently self-directed in their respective duties in the household of faith while living out their ministries in the world. But the demands of ministry and the peculiar relationship of pastors with parishes (employee/employer; leader/follower; servant/master?) requires that pastors belong to other kinds of communities within which they might openly share ideas, hopes, and fears about the practice of ministry.

Philip Amerson thinks modeling for such communities of shared practice must begin within the context of seminary education. He and his colleagues at Garrett-Evangelical Seminary are mindful of the value of "open space for those things—learning to think; growing in relationship skills—to happen with the seminary community. We are preparing pastors to work in real human communities, and preparation for this happens in the clear space in the seminary."[15] So they strive to create the conditions for lively Christian community in shared meals and the social entrepreneurship of a coffee house that serves as an alternative student center. And they provide vocational formation groups for students to test their own vocational clarity and to reflect on field work. These peer experiences pave the way, Amerson believes, for continuing peer and mentoring experiences once the students leave the seminary.

The importance of peer learning and support for effective pastoral leadership must not be understated. The study of the impact of peer support groups conducted by Austin Seminary, cited in the previous chapter, provides compelling evidence about the value of

such experiences. While John Wimmer sees the value of the collegial relationship between pastor and congregation, he is convinced
that peer groups are a crucial forum within which competence is
extended, agency is encouraged, and accountability is lived out.
He says, "The communities of competent shared practice help
ministers become knowledgeable about and disciplined in their
practice—to be able to do the job."[16] He is clear, having seen the
findings of countless projects across the country, that such peer
groups are one of the essential resources for sustaining pastoral
excellence. And he is further convinced that making such resources
available to pastors is a crucial task of the larger church. Most
important, he underscores the fact that actively sharing and pursuing growth in faith and practice do not replace trusting in God's
providence, a theme to which we shall return later in this chapter.

  This emphasis on mutual support for ministry is not an entirely
new idea, of course. Christian leaders have sought to encourage and
learn from one another ever since the eleven disciples huddled together in those agonizingly uncertain hours after the death of Jesus
on the cross. In his letters, Paul often pointed to the need for shared
practice. Roy Oswald and others in recent years have been writing and teaching about the importance of pastors' building support
systems for themselves, and Oswald's classic book *How to Build a
Support System for Your Ministry*[17] still offers useful guidance for
this endeavor. And a wide range of programs in the secular world,
including commercial efforts such as "Vistage," an executive and
leadership coaching program, and less structured groups such as
Parker Palmer's "circles of trust," have encouraged business, edu-
cational, and nonprofit leaders to form small groups of peers to
share personal stories and in some cases to follow more prescribed
curricula aimed at enhancing leadership effectiveness. What is new,
however, is the increasing data from research attesting to the value
of such groups for pastoral leaders and suggesting what works best.
What is also new, I think and hope, is the increasing awareness in
mainline churches that the larger church's role must become less focused on defining and enforcing rules and bureaucratic procedures,
and more aimed at empowering agency for pastors. Accountability
is still necessary, but the gifts and relationships of pastors can surely

be strengthened as they join with their peers to learn and grow in competent shared practice of ministry.

All of the pastors described in this book have been part of such communities of practice with peers and mentors at some point, and some have been part of these efforts throughout their ministries. Participation in such groups is one part of their stewardship of self that has equipped them for ministry over the long haul and that has helped produce the enduring fruit of their work. Such self-care is as important to the ecology of ministry as weeding and watering are to a garden.

Stewardship of self

Pastors rarely misunderstand the mandate to love God and love neighbor, but they too often fail to grasp the full meaning of the command to "love your neighbor as yourself." Jesus did not say "instead of yourself." I suspect this misunderstanding is most often rooted in some misguided attempt to live sacrificially, although I fear it is frequently a works-driven quest for worth or reward that instead bears witness to a lack of trust in God's grace. In my counseling practice I've seen hundreds of pastors over the years whose depression, physical maladies, spiritual burnout, and troubled family lives reflect their failure to love themselves as they love others. The ecology of ministry, like the ecology of our natural world, must include care for the person of the minister—body, mind, spirit, and relationships. While Jesus's warning in the Gospel of Matthew about bad trees' bearing bad fruit was aimed at the dangers of false prophets (Matt. 7:15–20), the logic of his metaphor could surely be extended to the importance of pastors' caring for themselves so that they might bear good fruit.

Physical health is one significant area of concern in pastors' self-care. A recent study conducted by the Clergy Health Initiative, for example, found that United Methodist clergy in North Carolina have higher rates of diabetes, arthritis, high blood pressure, angina, and asthma than do other demographically comparable people in the state. Nearly 40 percent of clergy met the criteria for obesity, compared to 29 percent of the general population. Other studies of clergy health have shown comparably troubling results.[18] My colleagues in pastoral counseling would report similar concerns about the frequency with which pastors struggle with mental-health issues and marital and family distress.

The Rev. Joel Garner, prior of the Roman Catholic Norbertine Community in New Mexico and collaborator with Sue in her work on clergy spiritual revitalization, points out that his brother priests are often struggling and overburdened. "Much of their time is eroded by things that have nothing to do with their fundamental vocation. There's no time for the intellectual life or spiritual reading. They have access to retreats and sabbaticals but don't take it. I think this is a big problem."[19] Father Garner thinks the larger church is too often neglecting the needs of clergy for support and rest, but "the bishops are so strapped for putting priests in parishes that they don't have time to send them off to further education." Clergy's need is part of what has fueled his longstanding ministry in spiritual renewal, and his community's establishment of its library and retreat house called Santa Maria de la Vid.

Harold Koenig, director of the Center for the Study of Religion/Spirituality and Health at Duke University Medical Center, and his colleagues conducted a review of research on mental-health issues among clergy because of their concern about the effect of low morale on vocational effectiveness. Their study sounded a serious alarm about self-care, especially among Protestant clergy, whom they found to have high work-related stress but few personal resources to cope with that stress.[20]

They cite a number of studies of clergy well-being indicating cause for concern about low self-esteem, fatigue, diminished marital satisfaction, and lack of social support among pastors across a wide range of traditions. The authors of this study recommend that priority be given to developing structures and support for greater self-care for ministers, beginning in seminary and continuing throughout professional life. It is encouraging to see seminaries and national church structures beginning to pay more heed to such recommendations.

Several good resources have been available for some time to pastors as they develop plans for better self-care. Rochelle Melander and Harold Eppley's book, *The Spiritual Leader's Guide to Self-Care*[21] is a sound and usable guide for understanding the issues involved in the minister's stewardship of self, and offers a number of useful strategies for maintaining a balanced life in ministry. G. Lloyd Rediger's *Fit to Be a Pastor*[22] outlines the need and catalogues some excellent tools for pastoral fitness, including physical, mental, and spiritual domains. Both of these books, along with continuing findings emerging from the Clergy Health Initiative at Duke Divinity School, chart an excellent course for pastors to follow in tending their personal vineyards. And as with most wellness and self-improvement programs, pastors who address these issues together with a group of their peers are more likely to see continuing positive results.

Russell (chapter 3) is one pastoral leader who has made an especially disciplined effort to maintain fitness so that his work might be strengthened. His regular exercise (especially running), careful eating habits, attention to marriage and family, and consistent involvement in continuing education all have helped support a long-lasting ministry. What's more, Russell and the other pastors in this book have all made good use of friendships, support groups, and structures of the larger church to help them weather the challenges and threats that are an inevitable part of living out God's call. In the process, they have also witnessed to a fundamental reality of Christian life and ministry: ours is a faith in community, and this faith bears fruit most bountifully when it is nurtured by and with others.

The other whose nurturance and companionship is most important, of course, is Christ. Koenig and his colleagues emphasize in their review of clergy wellness that spiritual self-care is at the heart of pastoral well-being. Sue's ministry is geared precisely to this priority, recognizing the essential truth of Jesus's words, "I am the vine, you are the branches. Those who abide in me and I in them bear much fruit, because apart from me you can do nothing" (John 15:5).

The vine and the vine grower

The word *ecology* was coined by zoologist Ernest Haeckel in the nineteenth century, bringing together the Greek word meaning "study of" with *oikos*, which means "house" or "dwelling place."[23] The ecology of Christian ministry is always surrounded by Christ. This is both a theological affirmation and a mandate for practice. Life in ministry must constantly be grounded in the lively practice of faith and confident hope in God's providence, even through the dark days of discouragement and loneliness that inevitably come for most pastors. Staying connected to the vine of Christ is the most essential task of pastoral leadership and sometimes the most challenging.

I always had some sort of religious belief, growing up in a minister's home—the home of two ministers, in fact, since both of my parents were ordained clergy. I remember as a child solemnly inviting my parents and sister into my room for evening devotions that I had planned in a most childishly pious ministerial manner. Church choir was a highlight of my childhood social life as well as a source of self-esteem, and for a time I proudly wore a three-year perfect-attendance pin for Sunday school. Staying connected to Christ was bred deeply within me.

Like many young people, I went through an adolescent period of angry rebellion before I experienced what I believed was a call to ministry at a summer church camp in Kentucky. A couple of times in my adult life I have had lover's quarrels with the church as I served as a minister in congregations and on our denomination's national staff, and as a pastoral counselor. But my faith has never left me entirely, despite an occasional detour. It has been sustained by stimulating and practical continuing education, good colleagues and friends in ministry, three spiritual directors at various times over the years, the imperfect dependability of the church, questions and epiphanies of counseling clients, and persistently curious reading in theology and spirituality. The past twenty years, though, have brought me to a more lively awareness and practice of faith than I could ever have imagined, fueled in part by some very dark nights. I have come to see that faith is the fundamental stock to which other ingredients of a pastoral life have been added. The texture and taste of that faith have changed markedly over the years, but the stock of the soup has been constant.

This transformation began, as I mentioned briefly in the previous chapter, when my friend Bill invited me to go off to a monastery with him for a week of silent retreat. I was living in central Missouri at the time, and I was clinically depressed. We had moved for my wife's new job as head of a church retreat and conference center, and for the first time in my adult life I was without a job or an established position in the community. I remember commiserating at a conference that year with a couple of other pastoral counselors who had also followed their wives to new locations, and we contemplated writing a book titled *Whither Thou Goest, Damnit!* I was lost and not coping very well. Oh, I was doing the appropriate things: taking medication, seeing a therapist, getting regular exercise. But Bill's invitation came as a siren song of health that touched something deep within my soul. I could not resist the lure.

Bill was one of the best leaders I knew. He was at the time president of our national professional association of pastoral counselors, and he had recently led his St. Louis pastoral counseling center through a stunningly successful period of growth that included building a beautiful office for the center's growing work. Bill had welcomed me warmly to Missouri and offered me a place in this new setting to work and belong. Only later did I learn that his own journey of faith had recently deepened when a friend had offered him a similar invitation to go on retreat. That renewed faithfulness, I think, was the quality in Bill to which I most responded.

We spent a week together in silence at Emery House in northern Massachusetts, embraced by the warm hospitality of the Anglican monks of the Society of Saint John the Evangelist. In the midst of that strange way of being together in silence, I learned, perhaps for the first time in my life, how to pray and to truly open myself to God's loving presence. As the river ice began to crack and melt in those warming March days, my icy heart began to warm to a new vision of ministry and faith. This new life was to be utterly dependent upon a providential vine grower and nurtured in a richly resourced ecology of ongoing spiritual direction and annual retreats, the love of a supportive and forgiving family, challenging ministry in a faith-based counseling center, and encouraging connection with peers and coworkers.

Bill's leadership in taking the initiative to invite me on that retreat has had a profound effect on my life, steering me into previously unexplored paths of faith where I have drunk from refreshing streams and glimpsed stunning vistas. He and I have gone on retreat together every year since. We don't talk with each other during the week, although we usually have plenty to share about our lives when we get together to prepare for retreat, and we always have lots to discuss after those five days of silence about how we see God working in our lives. Supported by the human companionship between us and the prayerful community of monks, the silence of the retreats enfolds each of us in our personal encounters with God. They are days of restful connection with the holy, sometimes wrestling with God's challenges, and usually finding direction for the weeks and years ahead. These annual retreats are an essential ingredient in my own mental health and my faithful leadership, and more than any other single practice, the retreats have helped me learn to be comfortable with leading a life based on faith in God's constant and generous care.

William H. Willimon, bishop of the North Alabama Conference of the United Methodist Church, has expressed concern about a recent trend in the church toward an emphasis on *practice* in the Christian life.[24] He fears that such a focus on practices "deflects our attention from the living God" and risks trivializing the power of faith into a series of activities reflecting mankind's attempt to wrest control of life and faith from God's hands into our own. I understand that concern and share it to some extent. My similar fear is that by telling stories of pastors whose ministries have borne lasting fruit, defining seven pathways toward enduring pastoral fruitfulness, and attempting to describe more fully the ecology of that ministry, I might be understood as suggesting that if pastors would just take better control of their professional lives they could be more successful.

While such initiative by pastors and the church might be helpful, my own experience contradicts this conclusion. The ecology of ministry, like global warming, may be profoundly shaped by human action, but it is ultimately in God's control. In two significant moments of my life God has reached out to me with the invitation to bear fruit—once as a green adolescent seeking direction and once as a wounded adult searching for new meaning. I have seen in my own life, and I am clear both theologically and pragmatically, that the formation of pastoral leaders is beyond precise human definition. How pastoral leaders bear fruit that lasts is ultimately a mysterious gift of God. Fruitfulness springs from tender and tangled branches watered and fed and pruned by the vine grower, the Creator who gracefully planted the vine from which the branches derive their capacity to bear fruit that is bountiful and enduring.

Seeds for a
Hopeful Future

These are perilous times for the church in the United States. Statistics on affiliation with a formal religion show that people are changing their connections more frequently, and formal membership in religious groups is declining, according to the Pew Forum on Religion & Public Life. Those who consider themselves Protestant now make up barely half the population, and only 18 percent count themselves part of mainline churches. While nearly a third of Americans were raised in the Roman Catholic Church, fewer than a fourth of adults described themselves as Catholic in recent surveys. Sixteen percent of Americans—almost one in seven—say they are unaffiliated with any religious tradition, more than double the number of those who say they were not affiliated as children.

While these shifts may indicate that people are actively searching for more meaningful spiritual lives, they may also reflect a decline in the church's vital life and witness. Leaders who can guide the church through these choppy waters will need to display courage, creativity, and careful attentiveness to the needs of people and to God's call. Some religious leaders despair of the depleted condition of our current crop of pastoral leaders. One seminary professor, for example, once told me that he believed seminary students these days brought with them more psychological problems and fewer intellectual resources than students in the generations that preceded them. Others cite American consumer culture's impact on the church as negative factor for clergy, echoing United Church of Christ pastor G. Jeffrey MacDonald's lament in a *New York Times* op-ed essay that many pastors feel as though they have been reduced to "the spiritual equivalent of concierges."[1] Craig Dykstra of Lilly Endowment has emphasized the urgent need for more effective pastoral leadership to address these disturbing trends:

> Particular congregations and the church as a whole can wither and die—or betray their calling—if they are not consistently fed and led by pastoral leadership possessed of the capacity to perceive, truthfully and deeply, through eyes of faith, what is actually going on in the world of which they are a part; to imagine what new life God is calling God's people to embrace; and to strengthen and enable the people to see it themselves and to live into it creatively.[2]

I do not think the church is about to die, although our confidence in resurrection would offer us hope even in the face of such a bleak future. But as church historian Philip Jenkins has extensively documented, the church around the world, especially in the Southern Hemisphere, is blossoming in amazing ways. Even in this country, pastoral leaders like those whose stories I've told in this book offer stirring testimony about the church's vital life and witness. These seven leaders, in fact, happen to be serving in just one medium-size city in the United States, and there are countless leaders like them in cities and towns across the country.

But the seven pastoral leaders described in this book are nearing the end of their careers, most of them having completed or nearing completion of more than twenty years in a single ministry. Some pessimists might even say that these excellent leaders are the last of a great generation and that "they don't make them like that anymore." I believe, though, that the future offers great hope, first of all because of the legacy these older pastors are leaving; they have cared for the fields well. The future offers great promise also because of young and energetic pastors like Matt, whose ministry

I described briefly in chapter 9. Such pastoral leaders continue to spring up like green shoots in fallow fields, enlivening communities with their joyful proclamation of the gospel and passionate efforts to embody their vision of God's reign on earth. And while seminary enrollment does show a growing number of older, second-career candidates pursuing ordination, a third of seminary students—the largest single age cohort—are under age thirty, and more than half of seminary students are still under forty.

Yesterday my wife and I worshiped at The Gathering, where thirty-two-year-old Matt is pastor. A hundred or so worshipers, most dressed in shorts, sandals, and casual shirts, gathered on a hot summer evening in the nearly hundred-year-old brick church building in an older urban neighborhood. A lively three-piece band played contemporary gospel music led by a young pianist with a soulful soprano voice as the congregation followed along with the words displayed on a video screen. The mostly under-forty crowd listened attentively to Matt's sermon, the first in a series titled "I Believe in God, but . . ." This one was "I Believe in God, but I Have Jesus Issues," and Matt delivered an engaging and solidly scriptural thirty-five-minute overview of Christology (yes, he used the word), sprinkled with references to Athanasius, heresies, sin, social justice, and a self-deprecating reference to his own premature baldness (receiving the appropriate laughs). It was a seeker sermon in a seeker service, but its intellectual depth and the solid liturgical structure of the service were quite different from the vapid caricature of such churches held by some mainline folk.

After communion was offered to all with prayerful graciousness and distributed with both efficiency and dignity, the laywoman who is director of discipleship asked for volunteers to help provide meals at a community social-service ministry and offered other opportunities to serve in the community. Matt invited people to talk with him after the service or to contact him by e-mail or on Facebook if they had questions about his sermon, or if they wished to join the discussion group meeting later in the week. Then, at the end of the one-hour service, he offered a benediction, and the worshipers headed out, stopping to chat with friends, to greet newcomers, or to visit with the "Connections Committee" members who had welcomed us in the vestibule with smiles and coffee or fruit smoothies when we arrived.

Sarah, a teacher in her early thirties, is delighted to find a church with this creative vitality, and she thinks Matt's leadership is the catalyst. "He listens, and he respects our new-generation thinking," she says. "His attitude of openness has helped the church provide a genuinely hospitable community in a sometimes anonymous city. He really gets it. And that allows us to develop the church in lots of exciting ways."

Matt founded The Gathering and has been its pastor for four years, having persuaded his bishop that a new-church start in this older section of the city was just what God wanted. It appears that he was right. And it also appears that Matt is bringing precisely the right qualities of leadership to this thriving ministry. Although the church was launched with a couple of dozen folks, now more than five hundred people worship every Sunday in the three services. It's too soon to tell, of course, whether Matt is bearing fruit that will last. But he surely is "bearing fruit with patient endurance" (Luke 8:15), while cooperating in the slow unfolding work of God.

Matt's leadership seems likely to endure because he's already walking the seven pathways we identified in chapter 9.

1. *Called to holy purpose.* He had long felt a call to encourage his denomination to start a new congregation in an aging urban neighborhood of his city where there were many churches, most of which were dying. Now that he is ministering just two miles from the college campus where that vision was born, this call remains a passion that drives his ministry and is bringing rapid growth and new believers to the church.

2. *Dependable authenticity.* Matt's warmth and transparent leadership, tempered by a growing awareness of the need for appropriate personal boundaries, is the kind of authenticity for which young people are yearning, he believes. He takes this genuineness one step further, noting that if he and the congregation are to survive and grow, the members "must move beyond my charisma and build an authenticity in the body itself."

3. *Trusting relationships.* He actively cultivates several intimate relationships of trust and mutual encouragement, beginning with

his wife of eleven years, Jessica. He and Jessica have a marriage counselor "on retainer," with whom they meet occasionally to help them keep their relationship growing. He has been meeting with a group of clergy peers every Tuesday morning for eight years to pray and study the lectionary and hold one another accountable. And he periodically seeks out mentors, wise experienced pastors and laypeople to whom he can go for advice and encouragement.

4. *A generous servant.* His commitment to being a servant leader is seen most clearly in such obviously heartfelt statements as this: "It's an honor that people let me sit up there and talk for thirty-five minutes about Christology." His gratitude about the opportunity to serve in ministry is palpable, and it comes out in statements like "I have great joy in doing this work."

5. *Creative adaptability.* The ministry of The Gathering clearly grows out of Matt's creativity, which draws from a variety of sources, including historic Christian and denominational tradition, evangelical experiments, and the resources of the modern secular world. One of his mottoes, which guides The Gathering's life, is "historically rooted and innovatively practiced." One of his metaphors for the ministry is to compare the church's operation to a fusion restaurant, tapping into the broad traditions of Roman Catholicism that are a major force in his city while blending in ingredients from his own denomination and other traditions.

6. *Disciplined persistence.* Matt has dreamed of leading this kind of ministry since he was a freshman in college, and once he was back from seminary it took two and a half years of planning and persuading church officials, bolstered by "the persistence of the Holy Spirit, to keep that vision alive." He also notes that his denomination can sometimes move very slowly, and so it took a certain amount of "institutional persistence," contending with bureaucratic barriers and occasionally nay-saying leaders, to bring his vision to reality. He is also clear that further persistence is needed as he continues to share this vision with others.

7. *Faithful spirituality.* When I talked with Matt after our recent visit to The Gathering, he told me that just the day before, he and his staff had been considering this question: "With all the new people, are we being intentional about helping them deepen spiritually?" Matt understands that strengthening the spiritual lives of

people in his congregation begins with attending to his own faith practices, which include devotional reading, a monastic style of praying together weekly with a small prayer group, and maintaining a balance between the very satisfying passions of his ministry and the passions of the rest of his life.

So long as God is raising up young leaders like Matt—and there are thousands of such ministers across the country and throughout the church—the fruits of the Spirit will continue to blossom in beauty and be harvested for the nourishment of all people. If we who love the church continue to tend the vineyard of pastoral leadership with care, helping to call forth future generations for such holy work, reasons for hope in God's promise will be well grounded. The church in all its manifestations must continue to devote innovative thinking and heroic energy to cultivating such leaders, creating a broad ecclesial culture of lifelong learning within diverse communities of shared practice that respect both the agency and accountability of pastors. And pastors themselves must exercise careful stewardship of their own gifts and cultivate their own spiritual vitality as faithful leaders called to high purpose. Out of such effort, deeply rooted in divine providence, will be borne the fruit of abundant life for all the world—fruit that lasts forever.

Notes

Preface. "Bear Fruit that Will Last"

1. Arlin Rothauge, *Sizing Up a Congregation for New Member Ministry* (New York: Episcopal Church Center, 1983). Rothauge discusses the structure, characteristics, relationships, and needs of four congregational sizes: family (up to 50 active members); pastoral (50–150); program (150–350); and corporation (350–500).

2. Henri J. M. Nouwen, *Lifesigns: Intimacy, Fecundity, and Ecstasy in Christian Perspective* (Garden City, N.Y.: Doubleday, 1986).

Chapter 1. Call to Fruitful Leadership

1. Debby Applegate, *The Most Famous Man in America: The Biography of Henry Ward Beecher* (New York: Doubleday, 2006).

2. Daniel Aleshire, speech to 2010 ATS New Presidents' Seminar in San Antonio, Texas, June 2010.

3. These data were reported in Jackson Carroll's definitive survey of contemporary Christian ministry, *God's Potters: Pastoral Leadership and the Shaping of Congregations* (Grand Rapids: Eerdmans, 2006).

4. James E. Kiefer, "For the Feast of All Saints, 1 November NT: A Litany of the Saints," *Biographical Sketches of Memorable Christians of the Past* (St. Albans, U.K.: Society of Archbishop Justus, 1999), http://justus.anglican.org/resources/bio/62.html (accessed June 1, 2010).

5. Brian McLaren, interview with the author, April 10, 2010.

6. Ronald A. Heifetz, *Leadership Without Easy Answers* (Cambridge, Mass.: Belknap Press, 1994).

7. These statistics come from an online article, "Report Examines the State of Mainline Protestant Churches" (Dec. 7, 2009). The full report is copyright © The Barna Group, Ltd., 2368 Eastman Ave., Unit 12, Ventura CA 93003.

8. The Rev. Joyce Lieberman, interview with the author, March 28, 2009.

9. Frederick Buechner, *Wishful Thinking: A Theological ABC* (New York: Harper & Row, 1973), 95.

10. Robert K. Greenleaf, *Servant Leadership: A Journey into the Nature of Legitimate Power and Greatness* (New York: Paulist Press, 1977).

11. Daniel Goleman, Richard Boyatzis, and Annie McKee, *Primal Leadership: Realizing the Power of Emotional Intelligence* (Boston: Harvard Business School Press, 2002).

12. Jim Collins, *Good to Great: Why Some Companies Make the Leap . . . and Others Don't* (New York: Harper Business, 2001).

13. N. Graham Standish, *Humble Leadership: Being Radically Open to God's Guidance and Grace* (Herndon, Va.: Alban Institute, 2007).

14. Roy M. Oswald and Otto Kroeger, *Personality Type and Religious Leadership* (Herndon, Va.: Alban Institute, 1998).

15. Parker J. Palmer, *A Hidden Wholeness: The Journey Toward an Undivided Life* (San Francisco: Jossey-Bass, 2004).

16. Richard L. Hester and Kelli Walker-Jones, *Know Your Story and Lead with It: The Power of Narrative in Clergy Leadership* (Herndon, Va.: Alban Institute, 2009).

17. Edwin Friedman, *Generation to Generation: Family Process in Church and Synagogue* (New York: Guilford Press, 1985).

18. Peter L. Steinke, *Congregational Leadership in Anxious Times: Being Calm and Courageous No Matter What* (Herndon, Va.: Alban Institute, 2006).

19. Margaret Wheatley, *Leadership and the New Science: Discovering Order in a Chaotic World* (San Francisco: Berrett-Koehler, 2006).

20. Tim Keel, *Intuitive Leadership: Embracing a Paradigm of Narrative, Metaphor, and Chaos* (Grand Rapids: Baker Books, 2007).

21. Max De Pree, *Leadership Is an Art* (New York: Dell, 1989), 11.

22. Stephen Covey, *The 7 Habits of Highly Effective People* (New York: Free Press, 1990).

23. James M. Kouzes and Barry Z. Posner, *Christian Reflections on the Leadership Challenge* (San Francisco: Jossey-Bass, 2004).

24. Heifetz, *Leadership Without Easy Answers*.

25. Nouwen, *Lifesigns*, 63.

26. Reported by Bob Burns and Rebecca Rine of Covenant Theological Seminary in the *Sustaining Pastoral Excellence* newsletter.

27. Fred Craddock, interview with the author, May 12, 2010.

28. L. Gregory Jones and Kevin Armstrong, *Resurrecting Excellence* (Grand Rapids: Eerdmans, 2006).

29. Craig Dykstra, speech delivered to a "Sustaining Pastoral Excellence" Forum, January 2004.

30. Jackson Carroll, *God's Potters: Pastoral Leadership and the Shaping of Congregations* (Grand Rapids: Eerdmans, 2006), 202–218.

31. David McAllister-Wilson, quoted in *Leading Ideas*, newsletter of the Lewis Center for Church Leadership, Nov. 9, 2005.

32. Craddock, interview with the author.

Chapter 2. *Richard:* Pastoral Integrity

1. Heifetz, *Leadership Without Easy Answers*, 14.

2. Jean-Pierre de Caussade, *Abandonment to Divine Providence*; trans. John Beevers (New York: Doubleday, 1975), 24.

3. Greenleaf, *Servant Leadership*, 13–14.

Chapter 3. *Russell:* Practicing Possibilities

1. Martin Seligman, University of Pennsylvania Positive Psychology Center website, www.ppc.sas.upenn.edu/.

2. Goleman, et al., *Primal Leadership*, 39.

Chapter 4. *Christine:* Building Resilience

1. That is, a parish with fifty or fewer members (see note 1, preface).

2. Salvatore R. Maddi and Suzanne C. Kobasa, "The Development of Hardiness," in *Stress and Coping: An Anthology*, 3rd ed.; Alan Monat and Richard S. Lazarus, eds. (New York: Columbia University Press, 1991).

3. Viktor E. Frankl, *Man's Search for Meaning: An Introduction to Logotherapy* (New York: Simon & Schuster, 1984).

4. Wheatley, *Leadership and the New Science*, 163.

Chapter 5. *Trey:* Passion for Justice

1. Trey's *Places of Promise Leader Guide* accompanies Cynthia Woolever and Deborah Bruce, *Places of Promise: Finding Strength in Your Congregation's Location* (Louisville: Westminster John Knox, 2008).

2. Saul Alinsky, *Rules for Radicals: A Pragmatic Primer for Realistic Radicals* (New York: Random House, 1971), 127–134.

3. Joseph Campbell, *Pathways to Bliss: Mythology and Personal Transformation* (Novato, Calif: New World Library, 2004).

4. Adam McHugh, "Can Introverts Lead?" *The Christian Century*, Nov. 17, 2009, 22ff,; excerpted from his book *Introverts in the Church: Finding our Place in an Extroverted Culture* (Downer's Grove, Ill.: IVP Books, 2009).

Chapter 6. *Carole:* Transforming the Story

1. That is, a parish of 50–150 members (see note 1, preface).

2. Justin Lewis-Anthony, *If You Meet George Herbert on the Road, Kill Him: Radically Re-thinking Priestly Ministry* (London: Mowbray, 2009).

3. Deborah Tannen, *You Just Don't Understand: Women and Men in Conversation* (New York: Ballantine Books, 1991).

4. Rowan Williams, from a 2004 speech at Ripon College in Wisconsin, quoted in Lewis-Anthony's *If You Meet George Herbert on the Road, Kill Him*, 81.

Chapter 7. *Sue:* Connecting with Spirit

1. Buechner, *Wishful Thinking*.

2. Palmer, *A Hidden Wholeness*, 58–59.

3. Warren Bennis, *On Becoming a Leader* (Cambridge, Mass.: Perseus Publishing, 2003), 104.

4. Standish, *Humble Leadership*, 18.

Chapter 8. *Paul:* Bestowing Blessing

1. Myron Madden, *Blessing: Giving the Gift of Power* (Nashville: Broadman, 1988).

2. Malcolm Gladwell, *Outliers: The Story of Success* (New York: Little, Brown, 2008), 267.

3. Kouzes and Posner, *The Leadership Challenge*, 225.

4. Ibid.

5. Graham N. Standish, *Becoming a Blessed Church: Forming a Church of Spiritual Purpose, Presence, and Power* (Herndon, Va.: Alban Institute, 2005), 118.

6. Ibid., 143.

Chapter 9. Pathways to Leadership that Lasts

1. Margaret Guenther, *Holy Listening: The Art of Spiritual Direction* (Boston: Cowley, 1992).

2. Charles Kimball, *When Religion Becomes Evil: Five Warning Signs* (New York: HarperCollins, 2002).

3. Rachel Maddow, www.smith.edu/collegerelations/com2010.php.

4. Bill George, *Authentic Leadership: Rediscovering the Secrets to Creating Lasting Value* (San Francisco: Jossey-Bass, 2003), 18.

5. Fred Craddock, interview with the author.

6. "A Study of the Effects of Participation in SPE Pastoral Leader Peer Groups," survey report and analysis, April 2010, available at www.austinseminary.edu on the College of Pastoral Leaders webpage.

7. Philip Amerson, interview with the author, July 8, 2010.

8. Greenleaf, *Servant Leadership,* 13–14.

9. Kazuo Ishiguro, *The Remains of the Day* (New York: Knopf, 1989), 245.

10. Sharon Watkins, interview with the author, June 24, 2010.

11. Bill Hybels, quoted by Diana Butler Bass in a blog on Beliefnet, October 30, 2007, www.blog.beliefnet.com/godspolitics/2007/10.

12. Janice Riggle Huie, interview with the author, July 16, 2010.

13. That is, a congregation of 150–350 members (see note 1, preface).

Chapter 10. Tending the Vineyard

1. Craig Dykstra, interview with the author, July 22, 2010.

2. Craig Dykstra, "Pastoral and Ecclesial Imagination," in *For Life Abundant—Practical Theology, Theological Education, and Christian Ministry*, Dorothy C. Bass and Craig Dykstra, eds. (Grand Rapids: Eerdmans, 2008), 41–42.

3. Ibid., 43.

4. Sharon Watkins, interview with the author, July 24, 2010.

5. Brian McLaren, interview with the author April 10, 2010.

6. Philip Amerson, interview with the author, July 8, 2010.

7. Charles Crutchfield, interview with the author, July 7, 2010.

8. Janice Riggle Huie, interview with the author, July 16, 2010.

9. Craig Dykstra, interview with the author, July 22, 2010.

10. Huie, interview with the author.

11. John Wimmer, interview with the author, July 7, 2010.

12. John Wimmer, presentation to Sustaining Pastoral Excellence Forum, Indianapolis, August 7, 2007.

13. Wimmer, interview with the author.

14. Wimmer, interview with the author.

15. Amerson, interview with the author.

16. Wimmer, interview with the author.

17. Roy M. Oswald, *How to Build a Support System for Your Ministry* (Herndon, Va.: Alban Institute, 1991).

18. Kate Rugani, "Body and Soul," on the Faith and Leadership website of Duke Divinity School, http://faithandleadership.com/features/articles/body-and-soul.

19. Joel Garner, interview with the author, July 15, 2010.

20. Andrew J. Weaver, David B. Larson, Kevin J. Flannelly, Carolyn L. Stapleton, and Harold Koenig, "Mental Health Issues Among Clergy and Other Religious Professionals: A Review of Research," *The Journal of Pastoral Care and Counseling* 56, No. 4 (Winter 2002): 393–403.

21. Rochelle Melander and Harold Eppley, *The Spiritual Leader's Guide to Self-Care* (Herndon, Va.: Alban Institute, 2002).

22. G. Lloyd Rediger, *Fit to be a Pastor: A Call to Physical, Mental, and Spiritual Fitness* (Louisville: Westminster John Knox, 2000).

23. Online Etymology Dictionary, copyright © 2010, Douglas Harper; found on dictionary.reference.com.

24. William H. Willimon, "Too Much Practice," *The Christian Century*, March 9, 2010, 22–25.

Conclusion. Seeds for a Hopeful Future

1. G. Jeffrey MacDonald, op-ed essay, *The New York Times*, August 7, 2010.

2. Dykstra, "Pastoral and Ecclesial Imagination," in *For Life Abundant*, 43.

Questions for Discussion and Reflection

While this book will have value for pastors who read it alone, the stories and ideas will have greater value when shared among colleagues. I would encourage you to gather a group of five to eight peers in ministry and read the book together, perhaps taking up a chapter a week. Then use these questions, or others that occur to you, to prompt your discussion together as you pray and consider implications for your own ministries. Whether you consider these questions individually or with a group of colleagues, I celebrate your continuing growth and fruitfulness in ministry. Thank you for responding to God's call.

Chapter 1. Call to Fruitful Leadership

1. What activities and accomplishments bring you the greatest satisfaction in your pastoral leadership? What are your greatest frustrations and causes for stress?

2. Who are your most significant models for pastoral leadership, and why?

3. What does "excellence" in ministry mean to you?

4. What fruits do you hope your pastoral leadership produces?

You and your colleagues may wish, as you begin working through this book, to set aside a larger block of time—perhaps even an overnight retreat—during which each of you has an hour or so to tell the story of your call to ministry and how your own leadership style has emerged in your work.

Chapter 2. *Richard:* Pastoral Integrity

1. How do you as a pastoral leader guide the parish to face its own problems?

2. Tell a story about the way you exercise authority as a pastor while still retaining an attitude of humility.

3. How have you helped people in your congregation exercise their own gifts and grow in their ministries?

4. How might people in your congregation describe the ways you are true to yourself and to your values?

Chapter 3. *Russell:* Practicing Possibilities

1. In what ways does your hope in possibilities affect your leadership?

2. How has the way you define and work toward goals in ministry grown and changed over the years?

3. What do you see as the benefits and liabilities of devoting much of your life to a long-term ministry?

4. In what experiences do you see a "resonance" in your relationship with your congregation and people in it?

5. How do you keep yourself fit—physically, emotionally, spiritually, and in your relationships?

Chapter 4. *Christine:* Building Resilience

1. What "seasoning" experiences of your life and ministry have fostered resilience in you and made you a better leader?

2. When have you been ready to give up on ministry? What contributed to that feeling, and what helped you move past it (if you did)?

3. What spiritual practices have been most helpful to you in learning to trust God's providence?

4. What experiences and people in your ministry have required your forgiveness?

5. In what ways have you as a leader helped your congregation make needed adaptations?

Chapter 5. *Trey:* Passion for Justice

1. Describe in one brief sentence your fundamental purpose in ministry.

2. In what ways is your pastoral leadership working to advance Christ's reign on earth?

3. How does your relational work as pastor contribute to accomplishing your goals as a pastoral leader?

4. Describe some of the ways you have taken "the view of the grandmother" in your leadership.

Chapter 6. *Carole:* Transforming the Story

1. In your practice of leadership, how do you attend to both numerical growth in your congregation and maturation in your congregants' faith?

2. What is your MBTI, and how does that fit with your congregation? (If you don't know much about the Meyers-Briggs Type Indicator, you might want to talk with a pastoral counselor or psychologist or personnel expert about taking the inventory, and even seeing if it might be useful in your work with congregational leaders.)

3. In what ways has your congregation's story changed under your leadership? How do those changes correspond with your own story?

4. How do you empower laypeople in your parish?

5. In what ways does your liturgical leadership inform your overall pastoral leadership?

Chapter 7. *Sue:* Connecting with Spirit

1. How does your extroversion or introversion affect the way you lead?

2. What practices help keep your spiritual life growing and lively? How do you "stay in shape" spiritually?

3. Do you see distinctive differences between the way women and men exercise pastoral leadership? If so, what have you noticed?

4. How do you allow yourself to be vulnerable in your ministry? What personal boundaries do you keep to set appropriate limits on your vulnerability?

5. How has your spiritual life waxed and waned over the years of your ministry?

Chapter 8. *Paul:* Bestowing Blessing

1. Who were the "fathers" and "mothers" who blessed you in your earlier life? How did they do it?

2. In what ways do you practice collegiality as a pastoral leader?

3. How do you mentor other Christian leaders? How do you "entrust"? How do you "equip"? How do you "encourage"?

4. In what ways is your leadership a blessing to your congregation and its members?

Chapter 9. Pathways to Leadership that Lasts

1. What are the roots of your own "holy purpose" in ministry? Does your purpose need to be modified in any way at this point in your life?

2. Describe some of the ways your authenticity comes through in your leadership.

3. How do you nurture trusting relationships, and with whom, in your life and leadership?

4. In what ways do you balance the call to be a servant in your ministry with the need to preserve your health and your individuality?

5. Can you identify a time when you creatively led your church through a truly adaptive change? If so, describe what happened and how you helped the church make the change.

6. How has your self-discipline enabled you to persist through challenging times and tasks?

7. What are some of the practices that help you keep your spiritual life as a pastoral leader vital and growing?

Chapter 10. Tending the Vineyard

1. What are the important elements of your "vineyard" that sustain and enrich your pastoral leadership? What's missing that you could add?

2. What should your congregation or denomination be doing that it is not now doing to "tend the vineyard"? How can you encourage that?

3. How do you cultivate your own lifelong learning?

4. What communities of shared practice support and challenge you?

5. What activities and attitudes help you be a good steward of self?

6. How do you see God reaching out to you in your ministry, and in what ways do you ensure your openness to God's initiative?

Recommended Resources

Here are some key books and resources on leadership and ministry that have shaped my views of excellence in pastoral leadership.

Books

Bass, Richard, ed. *Leadership in Congregations*. Herndon, Va.: Alban Institute, 2007.

> A collection of the some of the best articles on pastoral leadership published over a ten-year period in the Alban Institute's excellent journal, *Congregations*.

Carroll, Jackson. *God's Potters: Pastoral Leadership and the Shaping of Congregations*. Grand Rapids: Eerdmans, 2006.

> Duke Divinity School emeritus professor Carroll's definitive study of contemporary Christian ministry is a treasure trove of data as well as an eloquent analysis of the challenges and opportunities for the church and its pastors.

Collins, Jim. *Good to Great: Why Some Companies Make the Leap . . . and Others Don't*. New York: HarperBusiness, 2001.

> Collins's carefully researched and compellingly written analysis of what makes certain businesses more effective than oth-

ers (even though some of those "great" companies have fallen from their pinnacles in recent years) remains filled with excellent guidance for all kinds of leaders. See also his separately published recent monograph, *Good to Great and the Social Sectors*.

De Caussade, Jean-Pierre. *Abandonment to Divine Providence*. Trans. John Beevers. New York: Doubleday, 1975.
This spiritual classic by an eighteenth-century French Jesuit invites people into a deeper trust in God's providence and beckons them to embrace "the sacrament of the present moment."

De Pree, Max. *Leadership Is an Art*. New York: Dell, 1989.
A powerful and personal description of leadership written out of the author's experience as CEO of the Herman Miller Chair company, this slim volume has influenced countless business and nonprofit leaders.

Friedman, Edwin. *Generation to Generation: Family Process in Church and Synagogue*. New York: Guilford Press, 1985.
Rabbi Friedman's application of family systems theory to the dynamics of pastors and congregations, groundbreaking at the time he wrote it, remains a useful guide to understanding religious systems.

George, Bill. *Authentic Leadership: Rediscovering the Secrets to Creating Lasting Value*. San Francisco: Jossey-Bass, 2003.
Business leader and author George focuses in this volume on principles he believes contribute to enduring value in organizations.

Goleman, Daniel, Richard Boyatzis, and Annie McKee. *Primal Leadership: Realizing the Power of Emotional Intelligence*. Boston: Harvard Business School Press, 2002.
Building on Goleman's innovative research published in *Emotional Intelligence*, Goleman and his collaborators here apply the insights from that work to the practice of effective organizational leadership.

Greenleaf, Robert K. *Servant Leadership: A Journey into the Nature of Legitimate Power and Greatness.* New York: Paulist Press, 1977.

Greenleaf was a Christian layman who spent most of his professional life in industry. His keen eye for values and his roots in Christian faith compelled him to write this classic book, which launched the modern servant-leadership movement.

Heifetz, Ronald A. *Leadership Without Easy Answers.* Cambridge, Mass.: Belknap Press of Harvard University Press, 1994.

Harvard's Heifetz goes beneath simple formulas for effective leadership into the fundamental changes in organization and perspective that must be made to accomplish truly adaptive change that brings enduring effects.

Hester, Richard L., and Kelli Walker-Jones. *Know Your Story and Lead with It: The Power of Narrative in Clergy Leadership.* Herndon, Va.: Alban Institute, 2009.

Out of their work in the "Sustaining Pastoral Excellence" program, Hester and Walker-Jones offer keen insights and practical guidance on incorporating a narrative approach to pastoral leadership.

Jones, L. Gregory, and Kevin R. Armstrong. *Resurrecting Excellence: Shaping Faithful Christian Ministry.* Grand Rapids: Eerdmans, 2006.

Jones and Armstrong have written a compelling theological foundation for training and practicing excellence in ministry.

Keel, Tim. *Intuitive Leadership: Embracing a Paradigm of Narrative, Metaphor, and Chaos.* Grand Rapids: Baker Books, 2007.

Founding pastor of the growing Jacob's Well church in Kansas City, Keel is a passionate voice from the emerging church movement.

Kouzes, James M., and Barry Z. Posner. *The Leadership Challenge,* 4th ed. San Francisco: Jossey-Bass, 2007.

Professors at Santa Clara University, Kouzes and Posner have written prolifically and well about the principles of effective leadership within a variety of organizational settings, including another slim volume, titled *Christian Reflections on the Leadership Challenge.*

Lewis-Anthony, Justin. *If You Meet George Herbert on the Road, Kill Him: Radically Re-Thinking Priestly Ministry.* London: Mowbray, 2009.

Anglican priest Lewis-Anthony contends with the myth of the all-competent beloved parish priest propagated by the writings of George Herbert in the seventeenth century, and offers a realistic re-visioning of pastoral effectiveness for the twenty-first century.

McLaren, Brian. *A New Kind of Christianity: Ten Questions that Are Transforming the Faith.* New York: HarperOne, 2010.

One of the leading spokesmen of the emerging church movement, McLaren here frames and responds to key questions of the Christian faith with which contemporary pastoral leaders must grapple.

Melander, Rochelle, and Harold Eppley. *The Spiritual Leader's Guide to Self-Care.* Herndon, Va.: Alban Institute, 2002.

A practical compendium of ideas and resources grounded in solid theory to assist spiritual leaders in their vital task of stewardship of self.

Nouwen, Henri J. M. *Lifesigns: Intimacy, Fecundity, and Ecstasy in Christian Perspective.* Garden City, N.Y.: Doubleday, 1986.

In characteristically brief but beautifully abundant style, Nouwen invites Christians into fruitful (in contrast to productive) life and ministry that is nurtured by joyful intimacy with others and God.

Oswald, Roy M. *How to Build a Support System for Your Ministry.* Herndon, Va.: Alban Institute, 1991.

Long-time Alban consultant Oswald has been training and consulting with clergy and church systems, and this 1991 volume on the importance of support systems for pastors still offers comprehensive and timely guidance for pastors.